If everyone won one,
and everyone won won one,
how many would be won
when everyone won won one?

You were won by one—won to Christ by someone who
became your friend and shared the best news of all with
you.

But have you won one?
Do you know how to win one?

This practical book will show you how to lovingly win
your friends for Christ.

Ron Rand has trained thousands of Christians in the
principles and methods of FRIENDS evangelism.

And through the pages of this book maybe your friends
can be won by one—you!

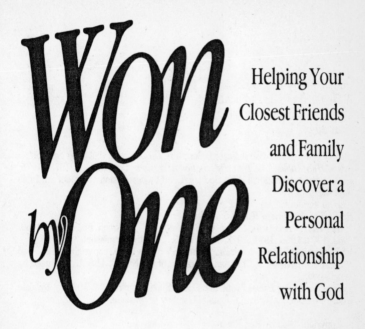

Won by One

Helping Your
Closest Friends
and Family
Discover a
Personal
Relationship
with God

DR. RON RAND

Regal Books

A Division of GL Publications
Ventura, California, U.S.A.

Published by Regal Books
A Division of GL Publications
Ventura, California 93006
Printed in U.S.A.

Library of Congress Cataloging-in-Publication Data

Rand, Ron, 1942-
    Won by one : helping your friends and those closest to you enjoy a relationship with Jesus Christ / Ron Rand.
        p.   cm.
    ISBN 0-8307-1238-0
    1. Witness bearing (Christianity) 2. Evangelistic work. I. Title.
BV4520.R34 1988
248'.5—dc19   88-11660
                                                                    CIP

1 2 3 4 5 6 7 8 9 10/ 91 90 89 88

Rights for publishing this book in other languages are contracted by Gospel Literature International (GLINT) foundation. GLINT also provides technical help for the adaptation, translation, and publishing of Bible study resources and books in scores of languages worldwide. For further information, contact GLINT, Post Office Box 488, Rosemead, California, 91770, U.S.A., or the publisher.

To the friends at First Presbyterian Church in Mora, Minnesota, where FRIENDS evangelism began.

To the friends at College Hill Presbyterian Church in Cincinnati, Ohio, where FRIENDS evangelism was refined and reproduced.

To Jennifer Marie, Joshua Christopher, Nathan Benjamin and Christopher Charles, family members who became friends through FRIENDS evangelism.

Contents

Special acknowledgments to George and Ann Bass, Jonathan and Jane Kopke, Suzanne Wade, Starr Luteri-Hicks and Ed Stewart, friends in Christ who made the FRIENDS manuscript come to life.

Find common ground with your friends. Witness through your common interests (see 1Cor. 9:19-23).

 Reveal your faith to your friends. Witness through your life-style. Earn the right to speak to your friends (see Jas. 2:14-17).

 Intercede for your friends. Witness through your prayers. Talk to God about your friends (see Col. 1:9).

 Express your faith to your friends. Witness through your lips. Talk to your friends about God (see Rom. 10:17).

 Nurture your friends through teaching, fellowship and prayer. Witness through your caring (see Acts 2:42).

 Disciple your friends to be followers of Jesus Christ. Witness through your intentional involvement in your friends' spiritual formation and development (see Matt. 28:19-20).

 Set your friends on a FRIENDS course with their friends. Witness by modeling how to "fish" for friends (see Mark 1:17).

CHAPTER 1
Let's Be Friends

I have been reminded of your sincere faith, which first lived in your grandmother Lois and in your mother Eunice and, I am persuaded, now lives in you also.
2 Timothy 1:5

Who shared the gospel with you? Who helped bring you into a personal relationship with Jesus Christ? As I look back on my life, it is very hard for me to identify exactly who was responsible for me becoming a disciple of Jesus Christ.

I remember going to the farm of my Czechoslovakian grandparents many times as a youngster. Every morning before breakfast I heard Grandpa Louis Vavrina read aloud from his Czech Bible and pray. Every evening I saw my Grandma Josie kneeling beside her bed to say her prayers. I often couldn't understand the words read or the prayers prayed. But I did understand that Jesus Christ was very important to my grandparents.

My father also prayed and read the Bible every morning. As an obstetrician, many times Dad would be out all night delivering babies. But even when he had little or no sleep, he would be in his chair with his Bible when I came downstairs in the morning. I also remember him telling about a difficult breach birth he attended. He said that he left the operating table for a moment and went to the window to ask the Lord for help. "Give me wisdom and skill," he prayed, "and let this woman relax." He then went back and delivered the child successfully.

When I was six years old, Dad took me with him to the city jail to care for an alcoholic. Dad had hired the man to do some painting in our kitchen, but he disappeared before completing the job. We later discovered that he got drunk, fell down in the street and gashed his head, and got picked up by the police. So Dad had to go to the jail and stitch up the wound. Instead of being angry, my father met the man with a smile, touched him lovingly and talked about how the Lord had been watching over him. I didn't understand how Dad could be so nice to a person who had looked and smelled so bad! But I did understand that my father even took Jesus with him into a jail.

My mother took my sister and me to church every week. Mom was always there to understand my problems as a growing boy. I could tell her anything and I knew that she would be accepting and understanding. She had insight and wisdom in every situation. My sister Ruth taught me the Lord's Prayer and encouraged me to memorize it. She told me how she talked about the Lord with her classmates and friends at school.

Links in the Chain

Outside my family, I was exposed to many other devoted

Christians long before I took the final step of consciously committing my life to Jesus Christ. I remember several Sunday School teachers who influenced me toward Christ. Jack Bannerman was a wiry bank president with a raspy voice. Although his career was in finances, Mr. Bannerman didn't put his trust in money. He was the one who taught me about tithing.

Another teacher, Fritz Finger, owned the local dime store. One time I was caught stealing some little Army tanks and I had to take them back to Mr. Finger and confess my sin. I remember his smile, his arm on my shoulder and his forgiveness. Whenever I saw him singing in the choir at our church I thought about those qualities.

There were other teachers—Homer Nelson, and the grocery store manager, and a farmer, and the woman who worked in the card shop. They all lived through the week what they taught me in Sunday School. And there was Rev. Given Kutz who came from the Pennsylvania Dutch country to be our pastor and became a good family friend. Our families took vacations together to Glacier National Park.

In the summer of 1956, Rev. Kutz invited Rev. Neal Kamp, the new Nazarene minister in town, to teach the junior high class in our Vacation Bible School (VBS). Rev. Kamp had a tremendous love for the Lord and a special way of relating to young people. Through the five days of VBS he explained very simply and clearly who Jesus Christ was and what He did for us by His death on the cross. On the last day of VBS, he gave us the opportunity to say a prayer that would seal a personal commitment to Christ. It was then that I consciously, willingly and joyfully turned my life over to Jesus.

Immediately after that prayer, I had to run uptown to present a reading for my mother at the Women's Association Luncheon. I was so moved by what had happened to me that morning that I asked permission to lead the group in prayer before the meal.

They were delighted. I don't remember the exact words of my prayer, but I know I mentioned that I had come to know Jesus as my Savior and Lord, and I invited others to do so as well. Then I thanked the Lord for the food!

That was my first witness—the same day I committed my life to Christ. I returned to Rev. Kamp after the luncheon and we spent most of the afternoon together talking about my commitment and studying the Scriptures.

So who led me to Christ? I believe all these people did. Each one was an important link in the chain leading to my personal decision. Rev. Kamp was the last link in the chain only because he was the one who summed up the gospel in a simple way and offered me an opportunity to pray.

Without a doubt, friendship and kinship evangelism is the most frequent means of introducing others to the church and to Jesus Christ.

I sincerely believe that any of my family members, teachers or friends could have done the same thing.

Every link in the chain is important. But it is the last link that makes the connection, binding a person by faith to Jesus Christ. This book will help you learn how you can be that last link, clearly and simply presenting to your friends and family members the opportunity to bind their lives to Jesus Christ.

A Witnessing Friend

What would you say if a friend asked you, "Why are you a Christian? What does it mean to have faith in Jesus Christ?" Could you open the Bible and explain God's method of transforming sinners into children of God? Could you explain in a simple, understandable way why Jesus died on the cross and how we can be forgiven for all our faults and live continually in a right relationship with God?

If you are terrified at the thought of explaining your Christian faith to someone else, you are not alone. Many people, both lay persons and clergy, do not know how to explain to someone what it means to have a personal relationship with Jesus Christ. Most Christians have never experienced the joy of bringing their closest friends, their spouse, or even their own children into a personal relationship with Christ.

The purpose of this book is to provide a variety of simple, easy-to-learn methods for sharing the Christian faith with those closest to us. These methods are based on seven principles summarized by the acrostic FRIENDS:

> **F**—*Find* common ground with your friends. Witness through your common interests (see 1 Cor. 9:19-23).
>
> **R**—*Reveal* your faith to your friends. Witness through your life-style. Earn the right to speak to your friends (see Jas. 2:14-17).
>
> **I**—*Intercede* for your friends. Witness through your prayers. Talk to God about your friends (see Col. 1:9).
>
> **E**—*Express* your faith to your friends. Witness

through your lips. Talk to your friends
about God (see Rom. 10:17).

N—*Nurture* your friends through teaching, fellowship and prayer. Witness through your
caring (see Acts 2:42).

D—*Disciple* your friends to be followers of
Jesus Christ. Witness through your intentional involvement in your friends' spiritual
formation and development (see Matt
28:19-20).

S—*Set* your friends on a FRIENDS course with
their friends. Witness by modeling how to
"fish" for friends (see Mark 1:17).

The most effective opportunities for sharing the good
news of Jesus Christ occur in personal relationships—
Christians honoring and serving Christ where they live.
When the FRIENDS principles are followed, the seeds of the
gospel find fertile soil in which to grow, mature and pro-
duce a harvest. These principles provide a framework that
allows friends to deal openly and honestly with the issues
of believing in Jesus and becoming His follower.

The primary emphasis of this book is training Christians to communicate their faith clearly and sensitively in
the natural context of personal relationships. The various
methods to be explained are extremely practical. They can
be used in day-to-day conversations without causing either
the one sharing or the one listening to feel awkward or
uncomfortable.

I Want to Be a Helper

Some years ago I joined several hundred church growth
information seekers to hear Win and Chip Arn expound

the characteristics of churches that had experienced significant membership growth in recent years.

One of the most startling statistics that the Arns communicated revealed why most people start attending a church. Sounding like an enthusiastic auctioneer seeking to raise the bid, Dr. Arn rattled off the following questions to those of us crowded into the conference room: How many of you began attending church because of a pastor? a special church program? the location of the church? the architecture of the church? a visitation ministry of the church? a family member or friend? Various numbers of hands were raised after each question. But guess which question drew the most affirmative responses—most convincingly so, without a doubt, without any need for a recount!

> *Introducing people to the church is one thing; introducing them to Jesus Christ is another. Churchianity and Christianity are two different issues.*

Think about your own situation. How did you first become acquainted with the church? If you are like over 90 percent of our group that afternoon, a family member or friend was your source of entry into the church. Without a doubt, friendship and kinship evangelism is the most frequent means of introducing others to the church and to Jesus Christ.

However, we cannot assume that the family members and friends who bring people into the church actually know how to introduce others to a personal relationship with Jesus Christ. Introducing people to the church is one thing; introducing them to Jesus Christ is another. Churchianity and Christianity are two different issues. I have conducted HELPER (*H*ow to *E*quip *L*ay *P*eople to *E*vangel-ize *R*egularly) seminars for more than 20 years in over 40 denominations and in several different countries. I have discovered that lay people in general do not know how to communicate their faith, especially through their words. The fact that the HELPER ministry continues to grow indi-cates a definite need to equip lay people for evangelism. When people learn how to be last links in the chain, we will indeed see a great harvest.

Proven Evangelism Principles

This book is written with both lay people and pastors in mind. It is for those who desire to share their faith and who desire to help teach others to do the same. It can be used as a textbook on personal evangelism in a church or school. This material has been used at College Hill Pres-byterian Church since 1973 to teach our entire member-ship practical methods for faith sharing. Our elders have deemed this material a prerequisite for church member-ship.

Our church shares what it has learned about FRIENDS evangelism in three HELPER seminars annually in Cincin-nati, Ohio, and at other national and international loca-tions. Our trained lay and ministerial team is available to provide HELPER seminars upon invitation from churches, seminaries or schools.

The principles of FRIENDS evangelism have evolved over years of practical experience in various witnessing settings. These principles have been tested and found effective in small and large communities, in rural and urban settings and in literate and illiterate cultures. These principles succeed because they are based on the practices of the early church as described in the New Testament, particularly the book of Acts.

Let me illustrate the effectiveness of FRIENDS evangelism by relating a couple of personal experiences.

A 10-year Friendship

I got to know Roger through his wife Lynn who had accepted Christ as her Savior in our new members' class. Roger was an executive for a local sports organization. I made no secret of being a rabid baseball fan and took every opportunity to speak with Roger about the sport (**F**— *Find* common ground).

Roger went to work early and came home late. He often took extended business trips and spent little time with Lynn or their two children. Lynn expressed to me her eagerness for Roger to alter his priorities and come to know Jesus. She asked me if I would talk to Roger about these issues.

"If I'm going to work with Roger," I told Lynn, "I think it would be best for me not to relate to him as a pastor, but to get to know him as a friend."

I asked Roger if we could meet for lunch on a regular basis—and I promised no God talk! He agreed. The first time we met it was obvious that Roger felt awkward about being seen with a minister. We went to a hole-in-the-wall restaurant with no windows and almost no lights. The place was downtown near Roger's office and he bought the lunch. A couple of weeks later he came out to my part of town and I bought the lunch.

As our relationship continued, I determined never to ask Roger for tickets to sporting events, even though I knew he had access to many complimentary tickets. I wanted him to know that our friendship was built on enjoyment of one another and not on what I could get from him (**R**—*Reveal* your faith. Witness through your life-style).

For more than 10 years I met regularly with Roger for lunch or breakfast. I found our friendship delightful because Roger wasn't a member of any church. I could be "real" with him in a way that it is sometimes difficult for a pastor to be with parishioners. I shared with him, without using names, some of the crazy situations pastors deal with. And he talked about the crazy situations in the sports business. We both gained insights into worlds that had been foreign to us. When we were together I stepped out of my "clergy" role and Roger took a break from being "professional." We were just ordinary guys. But all through these years I prayed for Roger, asking the Holy Spirit to prepare Roger's heart to receive God's love (**I**— *Intercede* for your friends).

One time we met at a swanky hotel for lunch and for some reason I decided to be bold. I said, "Roger, I think we're good enough friends for me to be up-front. If ever you were to tell me that your marriage was in trouble and that you were facing a divorce, I wouldn't be surprised. In my opinion, you are married to your business more truly than you are married to Lynn. But I want you to know that if you did get a divorce, it wouldn't change our friendship at all. I want to be your friend no matter what happens or whatever your future might be."

I will never forget the expression on Roger's face. He looked like a boxer who had taken two quick jabs in the jaw. He folded his napkin carefully and set it beside his plate. Then he looked up at me and said quietly, "All right. Thank you." And that was the end of the conversation.

Our friendship continued to grow. Then about five

years later Roger called me unexpectedly. I could tell by his voice that something was wrong.

"Ron, I need to see you, maybe even this afternoon."

"Sure, Roger, come on over. I'll clear my schedule."

When Roger walked into my office he looked terrible. "A long time ago you told me that if I ever got a divorce, it wouldn't change our friendship," he began. "I hope you still mean that."

I put my arm around him and he began to weep. He poured out his anguish for more than an hour—his failures, his unkept promises, his self-contempt. Exhausted and emotionally drained, he slumped back in his chair. "What do I do, Ron?" he sighed. "What do I do?"

I assured Roger again of our friendship. I picked up a New Testament and said, "Roger, the answer is in here. Do you want to look at it with me?" He nodded and I began to share (E—*Express* your faith. Witness through your lips).

It wasn't long before my friend Roger was on his knees, putting his trust in Jesus Christ as his Savior. The burden of guilt for his past failure lifted, but he realized that it still might be too late to save his marriage. I agreed and told him that he would need to trust in Christ completely for either the healing of the relationship or for strength to face the consequences of his past. I assured him that, whatever happened, God's love would not desert him and I would still be his friend (N—*Nurture* your friends).

Now, over a year later, Roger and Lynn are still together. It still may be a long time before some of the concerns in their marriage are completely healed. Roger left the job he was "married" to and took a position that gives him time to court Lynn and win back her love. He comes home early and, instead of sitting in front of the television, they go for walks or sit together in their family room talking. Roger told me that he had ignored Lynn for so long that he had forgotten what a beautiful, fascinating woman she was! He has been reading the Bible regularly and memorizing verses. He has also become involved in a men's Bible study and fellowship group (**D**—*Disciple* your friends to be followers of Jesus Christ).

Roger feels like a man who has been released after being held hostage for years in a foreign land. Now that he is free and has returned home, there are years of love to catch up on. Roger and Lynn are building a new family based on a new foundation. Both of them are sharing their experience with others. They even testified before our congregation (**S**—*Set* your friends on a FRIENDS course with others).

What a joy it was for me to see the value of a 10-year friendship when it came to revealing the good news in a "bad news" situation. Friendships earn us the right to speak and be heard.

Our aim in personal evangelism should not be to win souls or to add notches to our Bibles for the converts we conquer. That attitude is not only unbiblical but dishonest. It views individuals only as objects to be won. Christian love demands that we care enough about others to build lasting relationships, even at great personal cost. FRIENDS evangelism builds bonds of genuine concern and caring so that our friends will truly desire to hear about the source of love in our lives. If caring is our theme, even social events can turn into spiritual encounters.

Friends in the Pits

I got to know car dealer Tom Jennings while we were

hunting geese together near Oscar, Kentucky (**F**—*Find* common ground). When you spend three days with a fellow in a goose pit without razors, showers or toothbrushes, you get to know one another pretty well! Tom and I laughed and talked and joked together. He taught me a goose-call which lured flocks of geese close so we could bag them. Tom decided that I was an okay guy for a preacher (**R**—*Reveal* your faith. Witness through your life-style).

As the days wore on, Tom began talking about the problems in his marriage. He had always been good at managing important decisions, particularly in his business, one of the leading car dealerships in Cincinnati. But his marriage was marked by confusion and complications. He was seeking advice, but he didn't want any Jesus-talk. Silently I asked God how to approach him with the good news (**I**—*Intercede* for your friends).

After a thoughtful moment I said, "Tom, if I were to bring my car into your maintenance department with rust spots, you could simply paint over those spots and the car would look better right away. But you and I both know that it wouldn't look good for long. Rust spots need to be cleaned down to the bare metal. That's the only way to fix rust spots correctly.

"Tom, do you want me to paint over the rust spots in your marriage or do you want to get to the root of the problem?"

Tom saw the connection easily. "I don't want a paint job," he answered. "I want a permanent solution."

"Then we're going to have to talk about Jesus even if that's not exactly what you want to hear," I said. "Before anything can be done about your relationship with your wife, we need to look at your relationship with the Lord." Tom consented, so I opened the Bible and told him about

God's love for him (**E**—*Express* your faith. Witness through your lips).

Tom began a personal relationship with Jesus Christ that day and his faith has been growing ever since (**N**—*Nurture* your friends). His decision to trust Christ changed his relationship with his wife and children. It also changed a lot of things at his business. Soon Tom began having Bible studies at his dealership with his employees. Even some of his customers attended occasionally (**D**—*Disciple* your friends). Many people have come to a personal knowledge of Jesus Christ through Tom's Bible studies. These new believers have also been trained and encouraged in discipleship (**S**—*Set* your friends on a FRIENDS course).

> *Jesus is the only way to the Father, but there are many ways to come to Jesus.*

What common ground do you already share with your unbelieving friends? How can you begin to sow the seeds of FRIENDS evangelism with them? The fields are ready for sowing. The sooner you begin to sow, the sooner the harvest will come.

Methods for Your Ministry

In the examples above, I gave you the overall picture of how my friendship with Roger and Tom laid the foundation for sharing the gospel with them. But I did not explain in detail how I verbally shared the gospel with them (**E**—*Express* your faith) when the time was right to do so. Nor did I outline Rev. Kamp's presentation which led me to receive Christ as a youth during VBS. In reality there are many good methods for leading your friends and family members into the Scriptures to discover God's love and salvation. Jesus is the only way to the Father, but there are many ways to come to Jesus.

I grew up in the snow country of North Dakota where the drifts often reached the rooftops. I learned as a youngster that each snowflake is unique in its intricate design. The same is true of people. Each person is different from all others as evidenced by our different fingerprints. This tells me that when it comes to sharing the gospel with others, we must be sensitive to individual needs. There is no one way to share the gospel with everyone.

I have also learned this lesson of diversity through my religious background. My grandparents were English and Scottish Roman Catholics and Czechoslovakian Presbyterians. As a child I attended a Federated church (Methodist-Presbyterian), an Armenian church and several Presbyterian churches. I experienced a variety of expressions of faith through a variety of denominations. Within each denomination and each individual congregation there is a variety of persons with a variety of needs. We need to be equipped with a variety of methods for sharing our faith, ways that celebrate and respect our many differences.

You have been touched by God's grace and you can be a channel of God's grace to others when you are taught to communicate your faith effectively. That's what this book is all about. It is your personal evangelism helper— providing a variety of methods for sharing Christ which can be used within the context of the FRIENDS principles. Choose and adapt the methods which best suit you and the individuals to whom you are ministering.

CHAPTER 2
Tools and Terms

*How, then, can they call on the one they
have not believed in?*

*And how can they believe in the one of
whom they have not heard? And how can
they hear without someone preaching to
them?* Romans 10:14

Jon, a member of our congregation, told me about his first
experience at hanging wallpaper. *No problem!* he thought
at first. *No muss, no fuss, no mess from paint spatters or
sticky brushes. What could be difficult about pasting paper
on a wall?* In his naive confidence Jon told his wife Janna to
go do the grocery shopping while he did the wallpapering
by himself.

Jon started at one corner and worked around the
room. When he reached a corner, he just folded the paper
into it and kept right on going. He didn't think about the
door until he reached it. "And I don't even want to talk
about the windows," he groaned during his description.

When Janna walked into the room, she made the

strangest sounds—sort of laughing and crying at the same time. Jon's well-meaning attempt at wallpapering was a disaster. He had jumped into the job without the plans, skills or tools needed to do the job correctly. Everything he had done had to be torn down and replaced.

Plan for Success

In the same way, plans, skills and tools are necessary for effective witnessing. Proverbs 29:18 says, "Where there is no vision, the people perish" (*KJV*). I can add to that a proverb from my own experience: "Where there is no plan, the vision perishes."

The Greek word *katartismos* means to equip, train or furnish with the necessities. It also means to prepare intellectually and experientially. Early in the New Testament church the apostles equipped (*katartismos*) the believers to do the work of the ministry while they devoted themselves to prayer and the ministry of the Word (see Acts 6:1-4). This distinction is more clearly seen in Ephesians 4:11,12: "And his gifts were that some should be . . . pastors and teachers, for the equipment of the saints, for the work of ministry, for building up the body of Christ" (*RSV*).

In 1969 two lay persons pointed out to me that few English translations of this passage accurately reflect what Paul meant. He chose two different Greek words—*pros* and *eis*—to express a difference in purpose between leaders and believers. Translating these words properly, we see that pastors are called to do the equipping and the saints, or lay persons, are specifically called to do the work of the ministry. Paul goes on to describe a three-fold equipping process in 2 Timothy 2:2: "And the things you have heard me say in the presence of many witnesses entrust to reliable men who will also be qualified to teach others."

Understanding this distinction has made a great difference in my ministry. I began to take the stance of an equipper rather than one who does all the work of the ministry. Instead of being the pastor who ministers to all, I have tried to be the pastor who trains others to minister to all. Over the years I have learned three important steps in this equipping process. First, the pastor leads in a particular area of ministry with a lay person observing. Second, the lay person leads in that area with the pastor observing. Third, the lay person continues the ministry as a leader with another lay person observing in order to learn also. This is the essence of disciple-making—pastors equipping believers to win and equip others.

I find it interesting that when the persecution of the early church broke out, "all except the apostles were scattered throughout Judea and Samaria . . . . Those who had been scattered preached the word wherever they went" (Acts 8:1,4). It was the lay people who were dispersed into action in the book of Acts, not the apostles. The book could be aptly renamed the "Acts of the Laity," especially from Acts 8:1 onward.

Basic Definitions

I have had the privilege of traveling all over our nation and in several foreign countries teaching pastors, lay persons and seminary students how to share their faith. In December of 1978 our team was in Brazil conducting a seminar for the Overseas Missionary Society. We learned from the Brazilian pastors that it is easy to get decisions for Christ

in Brazil. But the difficult challenge is to build disciples out
of those who make decisions.

The goal of FRIENDS evangelism is to build disciples.
Evangelism does not end with a decision for Christ. Our
Lord's great commission clearly states that our witnessing
is only part of the process of making disciples. The methods and strategies outlined in this book are the tools and
training for effective evangelism and disciple-making. But
in order to understand the methods to be discussed, some
basic definitions must be presented. I hope this explanation of terms will help us avoid any confusion as we consider the art of FRIENDS evangelism.

What Is a Christian? A Christian is someone who has
been brought into a personal relationship with God by
grace through faith in Jesus Christ and in His work of reconciliation. When the Bible speaks about the intimacy of a
close, personal relationship it uses the word "know." Genesis 4:1 says, "Adam knew Eve his wife, and she con-
ceived and bore Cain" (*RSV*). The word "knew" in
Hebrew is *yada*. The meaning in this context is clearly intimate intercourse.

Now look at how Paul used the equivalent of *yada* in
the New Testament: "I consider everything a loss compared to the surpassing greatness of knowing Christ Jesus
my Lord, for whose sake I have lost all things. . . . I want
to know Christ and the power of his resurrection and the
fellowship of sharing in his sufferings" (Phil. 3:8,10). Paul
was a Christian who was not only involved in the work of
spreading the gospel, but who also pursued an intimate
relationship with Jesus Christ. A Christian is one who
knows Jesus intimately. As a result of that intimate relationship, a Christian shares in the work of Christ—the
ministry of service to others.

Romans 5:11 in the *Living Bible* describes the personal nature of our relationship with God: "Now we rejoice in our wonderful new relationship with God—all because of what our Lord Jesus Christ has done in dying for our

A few Christians are evangelists, but all Christians are called to be witnesses.

sins—making us friends of God." God calls us to personal friendship with Him. We grow closer to our personal friends as we spend time talking, working, playing and living with them. In the same way, the Christian has a growing, living relationship with the Lord.

What Is Evangelism? Evangelism is the activity of proclaiming the good news of Jesus Christ in the power of the Holy Spirit, through both our lives and our lips, so that others may believe in Jesus Christ as Savior and serve Him as Lord. The good news may be revealed by either an evangelist or by a witness. The word "evangelist" is used only three times in the Scriptures referencing certain gifted believers (see Eph. 4:11; Acts 21:8; 2 Tim. 4:5). The word "witness" is used many times in reference to all believers. In Acts 1:8, Christ referred to all believers when He said, "You will be my witnesses."

A few Christians are evangelists, but all Christians are called to be witnesses. One may be a witness without being an evangelist, but one cannot be an evangelist without being a witness. Witnessing is to be characteristic of all who have placed their trust in Jesus Christ. You witness to the fact that Jesus Christ is Lord simply by accepting the name "Christian." You cannot be a Christian without being a witness. Here is where the *E* of FRIENDS evangelism is activated. As witnesses we express with our lips the good news so our friends will understand that they too can know Jesus Christ intimately.

I went to the Mora Presbyterian Church in Minneapolis straight out of seminary. As a seminarian I studied Greek under Floyd Filson, one of the great New Testa-

Evangelism is the gift of the Spirit for some,
but witnessing is the gab of the Spirit for all.

ment scholars of the twentieth century. But it was Wes Rydell, a lay person in the Mora Church with only a high school education, who pointed out to me the biblical difference between an evangelist and a witness. Wes's insight helped me realize that evangelism is the *gift* of the Spirit for some, but witnessing is the *gab* of the Spirit for all.

The word "witness" comes from the Greek word which gives us our word "martyr." The implication is that Christian witnesses are to be martyrs, not only in the sense of suffering or dying as the word later came to mean, but by earning the right to be heard by laying our lives down daily in service of others.

Evangelism can only happen in the power of the Holy Spirit. Jesus said, "You will receive power when the Holy Spirit comes on you; and you will be my witnesses" (Acts 1:8). It is the dynamic of the Holy Spirit that enables us to witness. He is the Enabler. God the Holy Spirit empowers and enables every one of us to be a witness just as he empowers some of us to be evangelists. It is most important for Christians to understand the source of their enabling if they are to communicate their faith effectively.

The Greek word for Spirit (*pneuma*) is the same as the word for wind. Have you ever tried to fly a kite without wind? Many Christians do not speak about their personal faith because they do not allow the holy wind of the Spirit to move them. Sometimes this is so because they do not understand the ministry of the Holy Spirit and the concept of being filled with the Spirit. This concept is described in greater detail later in the book.

The fear of what others think keeps many Christians from telling the good news. We are afraid we will offend others, or appear "different" and be labeled religious fanatics. And so we remain secret-service Christians like Joseph of Arimathea who "was a disciple of Jesus, but secretly because he feared the Jews" (John 19:38).

Fear of others fades with the empowering of the Holy Spirit, with training in evangelism and with experience. Fear also fades as we introduce our unbelieving friends to other Christians. When we include our friends in Christian fellowship and celebration, they will see a community of Christians who share the faith and happiness in Jesus Christ we are proclaiming.

There is more to witnessing than living a good life. Witnessing requires a Spirit-empowered presentation of the spoken word. Paul said, "Faith comes by hearing the message" (Rom. 10:17). Witnessing by one's life-style only is not enough because our walk does not always match up with our Christian standards. Even Peter and Paul, whose lives are recorded in Scripture as examples for us, were not 100 percent perfect. They pointed toward the only Perfect One, Jesus Christ, with their words as well as with their lives.

What Is a Witness? Let's compare witnessing for Christ with witnessing in a court of law. There are two major characteristics of an effective courtroom witness, but there are at least three characteristics required of a Christian witness.

First, a witness must possess good character. In court, a witness must be able to demonstrate a reputable character before his or her testimony will be accepted. Likewise, the character of a Christian witness must be consistent. When we want to share the good news with our friends, we must demonstrate reputable character by being a friend at all times and in all circumstances. If we are available for people when they need a friend, they will know that our testimony is reliable.

Second, a witness must have seen or experienced something. The perspective or interpretation of an event may be slightly different from witness to witness. But the testimony of a witness is considered valid if it is consistent with the established facts. Matthew, Mark, Luke and John all experienced Jesus from different perspectives and each described the same events from his own point of view. But each one is a trustworthy witness. Christian witnesses must testify about their personal experience with Christ.

If someone witnessed a crime and was called to the witness stand, but refused to say anything, that person would not be a witness. Instead, he could be held in contempt of court. This was vividly exemplified in Cincinnati several years ago when a pastor was charged with aiding the escape of three inmates from a local correctional center. The pastor, a man of reputable character, witnessed a portion of the escape. But when subpoenaed to appear before the grand jury, he refused to testify. The pastor was sentenced to 111 days in jail for contempt of court.

Each Christian is continually on the witness stand. We are called to testify about the reality of Jesus Christ in our lives. Our good reputation is not enough. We *must* speak out.

Finally, a Christian witness must be filled with the Holy Spirit. It is interesting to note that the witness of words often follows the phrase "filled with the Holy Spirit" in the New Testament: "You will receive power when the Holy Spirit comes on you; and you will be my witnesses . . . " (Acts 1:8); "Then Peter, filled with the Holy Spirit,

It is the filling of the Holy Spirit that moves us to speak to the proper person at the proper time in a proper manner.

said . . . " (Acts 4:8); "They were all filled with the Holy Spirit and spoke . . . " (Acts 4:31); "Be filled with the Spirit.

"Speak to one another . . ." (Eph. 5:18,19). And Jesus encouraged His disciples in their testimony when He said: "Whenever you are arrested and brought to trial . . . say whatever is given you at the time, for it is not you speaking, but the Holy Spirit" (Mark 13:11).

It is the filling of the Holy Spirit that moves us to speak to the proper person at the proper time in a proper manner. And this is only natural since it is the Holy Spirit who will move in that person's heart, causing a response in faith to the good news.

FRIENDS evangelism emphasizes that we express our faith with sensitivity. To paraphrase Solomon's words, there is a time to speak and a time to shut up! We are to witness boldly, but not inappropriately. A witnessing friend recognizes when it is proper to speak and when it is improper. A fruit of the Spirit is self-control. Being filled with the Spirit will equip us to exercise self-control over insensitivity in witnessing.

Jesus said, "No one can come to me unless the Father who sent me draws him, and I will raise him up at the last day" (John 6:44). In all our witnessing we must remember that God the Father is the supreme evangelist. The early Church understood this principle as evidenced by Luke's record in Acts 2:47: "And the Lord added to their number daily those who were being saved." God was the prime factor in the growth of the early Church.

Paul clarified our partnership role with God in witnessing when he said: "We are therefore Christ's ambassadors, as though God were making his appeal through us" (2 Cor. 5:20). Our responsibility is to witness in the power of the Holy Spirit and then leave the results to God. He is the Lord of the harvest.

In FRIENDS evangelism, the second principle—reveal your faith to your friends—encompasses the ministry of compassionate service. Would a friend see a friend hungry and not buy her groceries? Would a friend refuse to offer a ride to the doctor if he has a car available? Wouldn't a friend try to meet the needs of a friend in every way?

A spiritual ministry without a social ministry is a spirit without a body—and that's an "unholy" ghost. A social ministry without a spiritual ministry is a body without a spirit—and that's a corpse. There is no such thing as a "traditional gospel" as opposed to a "social gospel." There is only one true, inclusive gospel which ministers compassionately to the whole person. It is only natural for Christians who have been born of the Spirit to be involved with others in a social ministry of compassion. Remember: Jesus came to serve, not to be served.

What Is Salvation? Paul informed us that God "wants all men to be saved and to come to a knowledge of the truth" (1 Tim. 2:4). The root of the word "salvation" is the Latin word *salvere* which denotes healing or the restoration of health and wholeness. God desires that all become whole in Jesus Christ—whole in body, mind and spirit. In

Jesus Christ the Great Physician, as the song says, "there is a balm in Gilead that heals the sin-sick soul."

Our salvation is both a product and a process. As a product, salvation was accomplished at Calvary when Christ "was pierced for our transgressions, he was crushed for our iniquities; the punishment that brought us peace was upon him, and by his wounds we are healed" (Isa. 53:5). As a process, salvation began when "God, who is rich in mercy, made us alive with Christ even when we were dead in transgressions. . . . For it is by grace you have been saved, through faith—and this not from yourselves, it is the gift of God—not by works, so that no one can boast" (Eph. 2:4,5,8,9).

Salvation stems from God and His work of grace in Jesus Christ. It does not stem from us, our works or efforts. This aspect of the process of salvation makes Christianity unique among the religions of the world which emphasize what people must do rather than what God has done. Salvation cannot be achieved; it can only be received.

But we have a role to play in the process of salvation. Our part is described in Romans 10:13-15: "'Everyone who calls on the name of the Lord will be saved.' How, then, can they call on the one they have not believed in? And how can they believe in the one of whom they have not heard? And how can they hear without someone preaching to them? And how can they preach unless they are sent?"

God uses people to form the vital links of the chain leading to salvation. Every time a Christian witnesses by life or lips another link is added. Finally the last link of personal commitment is formed. The chain becomes complete and links God with another person. When we proclaim Christ and extend an invitation to others to receive

Him, we often have the privilege of being the last link God uses in this process.

Not long ago while hunting ducks on the Ohio River, I observed several boats moving between two bodies of water through a series of locks. The boats ascended from the lower level to the higher level when water was released from above into the level that the boat occupied.

The process of salvation can be compared to this process. The boats represent individuals and the locks represent the stages of the salvation process. A person ascends from one level to another when the Living Water is released into the person's present level of understanding of Christianity. Just as the boats are dependent on the water to move upward, so individuals are dependent on the Holy Spirit, the Living Water. (See illustration on next page.)

The critical step of personal commitment occurs when an individual moves from the Action level to the Unity with God level. At that point a person says something like, "I give as much of myself as I know of myself to as much of Christ as I understand about Christ." This broad commitment allows for continuous growth and change.

For some individuals, the commitment experience is sudden and spectacular, a lightning bolt event such as the conversion experience of the apostle Paul in Acts 9. For others, it is a gradual experience like that of Nicodemus. In John 3 Nicodemus was totally unaware of the plan of salvation. In John 7 he was somewhat aware of who Jesus was. But in John 19 Nicodemus clearly took an action step and committed himself to Jesus Christ by participating in His burial. The depth of his commitment becomes apparent when we realize that Nicodemus knew the Jewish law which prohibited Jews from touching dead bodies. According to the letter of the law, Nicodemus would be ceremoni-

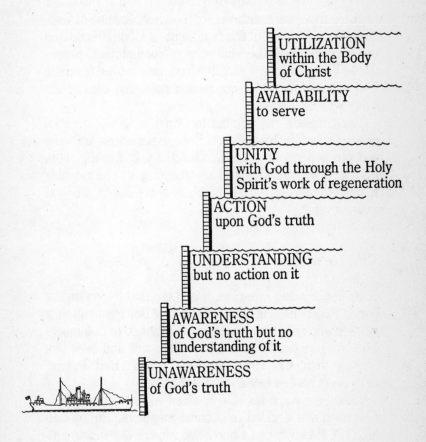

UTILIZATION
within the Body
of Christ

AVAILABILITY
to serve

UNITY
with God through the Holy
Spirit's work of regeneration

ACTION
upon God's truth

UNDERSTANDING
but no action on it

AWARENESS
of God's truth but no
understanding of it

UNAWARENESS
of God's truth

ally unclean after touching Jesus' body and thus unable to participate in the Passover celebration. While the other Jewish people were partaking of the symbolic lamb of God, Nicodemus partook of the real Lamb of God. He counted the cost and took the vital step of commitment. Somewhere between John 7 and 19 Nicodemus moved from the Understanding stage to the Action stage and then to the Unity with God stage.

Your friends may commit to Christ suddenly like Paul or gradually like Nicodemus. Both experiences are valid and are dependent upon God's activity in moving them from level to level. Our goal in witnessing is to be available to be used by God—and available to serve our friends—at every level.

The New Red Penny

"Breaker, breaker one-nine, this is the Red Penny on the line." "Red Penny" is the CB handle for Bob Pennington, a trucker who drives the route from Cincinnati to Columbus. The truckers on that route know him well and seek him out on their CB channels. He's called "Red Penny" because of his red hair and his last name.

Red Penny and his wife Evaleen visited our church in Cincinnati and decided to become members. But at College Hill Presbyterian Church we require our new members to take a 10-week new member's class which includes our FRIENDS evangelism training. Being on the road two or three weekends each month, Red Penny just couldn't work the classes into his schedule. So we agreed that he would listen to the new member's class sessions on cassette tapes as he traveled.

The first tape in the series explains the meaning of sal-

vation and ends with an invitation and a prayer. As Red
Penny listened, he realized that he had never believed in
Jesus Christ as his own Savior. So as the tape ended he
pulled his truck to the shoulder of the highway, prayed and
gave his life to Jesus Christ.

When he returned to Cincinnati a few days later he
called me to tell me what had happened. We rejoiced
together over the phone. "I left more than a load of cargo
on that trip to Columbus," he bubbled. "I dropped off a
whole lifetime of sin and I came back to Cincinnati carrying
a truckload of joy and peace." Amen!

For Better or Worse

As a pastor I often counsel engaged couples. When I do, I
make certain that they understand the difference between
the wedding and the marriage. The wedding is a one-day
event—it's exciting, happy and fun. But the marriage is a
day after day after day experience. Some days will be
exciting and fun, but others will be dull, difficult or awful.
That's just part of marriage.

It is much easier to say "I do" at the wedding than it is
to build the marriage month by month, year by year.
That's why I also make certain that the engaged couples
include Jesus Christ in their marriage. They need His
faithfulness to remain faithful to each other "for better or
for worse."

I remember one sad encounter with a married couple
who came to me for counseling. The wife was gaunt and
her long blond hair hung in lank strands around her emaci-
ated face. Her movements and speech were slow and
deliberate. The husband was muscular, handsome and
lively, with thick black hair and broad shoulders. He looked

like an athlete; she looked like the memory of better days.

She had been a high school homecoming queen and he had been a football star. Both were among the most popular students on campus. They were the perfect couple—the cheerleader and the quarterback—the stars of a storybook romance and marriage.

But six weeks after the wedding her cover girl beauty was permanently marred in a near-fatal automobile accident. Though badly scarred and crippled, she delighted the doctors and therapists with her recovery. Only two-and-a-half years after the accident she was able to walk, speak and care for herself without much assistance.

But she was different. She looked like she was in her 60s. She was no longer the beauty queen her husband had married. He was not prepared for the long process of recuperation or the reality of living with a handicapped spouse.

"I'm still a young man," he said. "I feel like a real jerk, a clod, a heel. But I would be lying to say I wanted to stay in this marriage. She's not the same woman I married. I don't want to spend my whole life like this. She will never be different than she is now. We can never do things together again, never have any fun. I want the freedom to be the person I really am. I want to share my life with someone who can enjoy it with me."

There was sorrow in my heart as that young man walked out of my office. On my request, the wife stayed with me a little longer and I listened as she struggled to express her sorrow. She said that she also wanted a divorce. She realized that what she thought was love had been shallow infatuation. Her husband had been in love with an image, not with her real self.

When we tell Jesus Christ that we want Him to be our Savior and Lord, we say by faith that we will trust Him from start to finish. We don't know what will happen tomorrow, but we know that He will be with us forever.

And, praise God, our security does not rest in our faithfulness, but in His faithfulness. He will remain with us through better and worse. This is part of the exciting good news we must share with our friends.

CHAPTER 3
Understanding Our Friends

*Those who are led by the Spirit of God are
sons of God* Romans 8:14

Bob Terry is a friend of mine who manages a supermarket
in a suburb north of Cincinnati. As a member of our
church, Bob has received FRIENDS evangelism training as
part of his preparation for membership.

A couple of years ago I asked Bob what he did when
shoplifters were caught in his store. He described the process of bringing offenders to his office, confronting them
with the evidence, calling the police, pressing charges and
then releasing them to the authorities. I suggested that
perhaps he might consider using his evangelism training as
a means of evangelizing shoplifters. What a captive audi-
ence! What an opportunity to speak about sin and forgiveness!

Bob laughed and nodded. "Why not?" he said. "What
have I got to lose?"

Shortly after our conversation Bob called me to say
that he had won his first repentant thief. The shoplifter

had been caught red-handed by some employees who brought him to Bob's office. Bob just looked at the man for a moment or two. The fellow was understandably uncomfortable, awaiting the justice he deserved. Then Bob took a paperback New Testament from his bookshelf and handed it to the shoplifter. "I want to give this to you as a gift," Bob said. Then he began sharing Scripture passages he learned during his FRIENDS evangelism training.

The shoplifter was absolutely overwhelmed! He accepted Jesus Christ as his Savior and left the supermarket a new person. He returned to Bob's store repeatedly, not to steal but to talk with Bob about his new faith. Soon the man told Bob that he and his wife had joined a church in the neighborhood.

Double Jeopardy

Over the years I have spent many seasons coaching Little League baseball in Cincinnati. I made a habit of presenting a short Bible study before each practice. More often than not the parents of my players would listen and participate. The city baseball director couldn't help but notice that I was personally involved with the families of my team members. He was delighted that I was reaching out to these people. So he went out of his way to place on my team boys and girls with divorced or separated parents, thinking that I could help them in some way.

The ultimate awkward situation occurred when Johnny Franklin was assigned to my team. Both his parents were divorced and remarried. Johnny's natural father was our first base coach and his stepfather was our third base coach. During practices and games I had to deal with the natural father on first base, the stepfather on third base and the mother and stepmother at opposite ends of the bleachers. Poor Johnny was literally stuck in the middle.

There were some tense moments dealing with these two families. But in spite of the awkwardness, I had the opportunity to help both couples work through several very delicate situations. They began to see what could be accomplished in the context of affirmation and friendship instead of condemnation and blame-fixing. As the weeks passed, the two couples gingerly risked communicating with each other when it was important for Johnny that they do so. Those "close encounters of a hot kind" were useful in planting seeds of hope and forgiveness.

Did I share the good news with these troubled people? Yes, through model and example. But no, I did not verbalize the gospel with either couple that season. I believe that I could have spoken with them about Jesus Christ because I had earned the right through being a friend to their son. Yet it did not seem right to do so. I prayed that they might take the initiative to ask about my faith, but they did not.

The Importance of Guidance

What do these two examples have in common? Both illustrate the need to be sensitive to the guidance of the Holy Spirit when speaking to others about the good news. Sometimes it is appropriate to share with friends when the opportunity is opened in a natural and sincere way. But sometimes sharing is inappropriate. It won't always be clear to us why the timing is not right, but it just "feels" wrong. I try to trust the Holy Spirit at these times because God knows the thoughts and heart of every person. If I insist on imposing a testimony on a person, maybe I could justify it to myself. But I risk driving that person further away from trusting in Jesus Christ. I am not out to "win souls," but to be a friend and seek to be a sensitive witness for my Lord.

Unfortunately I sometimes fail to act upon the discernment of the Spirit. For example, once I was standing with my son Nathan in the check-out lane of a busy discount store. As we waited for the clerk serve the customer ahead of us, we heard a woman behind us read aloud to her friend the latest tabloid headline: "Life After Death Guaranteed!" The other woman laughed and commented that no one could guarantee life after death.

I looked at Nathan and he looked at me. I slipped my hand into my pocket where I keep a small New Testament and a few miniature crosses to use as tools in witnessing. But I didn't say anything. In a moment the women's conversation changed and it was my turn at the cash register.

I could have said to those women, "I couldn't help overhearing you. I don't know what this tabloid says, but I do know what the Bible says. There is someone who can give us a guarantee of eternal life." But I didn't. By the time we passed through the check-out lane the opportunity was gone. I felt the prompting of the Holy Spirit but I chose not to say anything. There will be times when we blow it. We can always choose to say no to the Spirit's prompting.

Three Kinds of Persons

The Bible reveals that there are only three kinds of persons living in the world. You can find all three in every country, race, creed and color. Each of us, and every person we meet, falls into one of these three categories.

All three kinds of persons are illustrated in 1 Corinthians 2:14—3:1: "The man without the Spirit does not accept the things that come from the Spirit of God . . . The spiritual man makes judgment about all things, but he himself is not subject to any man's judgment. . . . Brothers, I could not address you as spiritual but as wordly—mere infants in Christ."

The Unspiritual Person. The first kind of person identified in verse 14 is not a Christian. "The man without the Spirit" cannot understand or accept spiritual things from God. Spiritual things sound foolish to that person because only those who have the Holy Spirit within them can understand spiritual things. God is Spirit and must be understood in the Spirit. The person who is not a Christian may have an intellectual knowledge of Christ, may be involved in the life of the church and may even know Jesus as a figure of history, a great teacher or the Son of God. But this person has not encountered Jesus Christ through the Holy Spirit. The indwelling Spirit has not entered this person's life.

The *Revised Standard Version* calls this person "unspiritual." The *King James Version* translates the same term "natural," born by nature into this world and in need of being born again. Each individual must have a spiritual birth to enter the spiritual life, just as one must have a physical birth to enter the natural life.

The Spiritual Person. The second kind of person is identified in verse 15 as "spiritual." This person has insight into everything and actually has a portion of the very thoughts and mind of Christ within. *The Living Bible* refers to spiritual persons as "healthy Christians, who are filled with the Spirit" (1 Cor. 3:1). The spiritual person is a Christian and is controlled by the mind of Christ. The

Christian knows Jesus as Savior and relates to Him as Lord.

Several members of our church joined me in Port-au-Prince, Haiti, to help train pastors and lay people in FRIENDS evangelism methods. While there I had an opportunity to go snorkling in a beautiful blue bay. I walked out to armpit depth in the water and looked down. Every once in awhile I would see a fish or two swim by. Then a missionary friend told me to put on the mask and lower my head into the water.

I followed his instructions and I was amazed! All of a sudden it seemed like I could see for miles under the water. There were dozens of kinds of fish, coral and sea shells all around me that I hadn't seen before. I had not moved a step or gone deeper. I simply put on the mask and lowered my head into the water.

That's what it's like when we put on the mind of Christ. Suddenly we see spiritual things through the eyes of the Spirit.

The Carnal Person. The third kind of person is identified in 1 Corinthians 3:1 and described in verses 2 and 3. The apostle Paul was writing to Christians, which literally means "Christ-in-ones." "Brothers, I could not address you as spiritual but as worldly—mere infants in Christ. I gave you milk, not solid food, for you were not yet ready for it. Indeed, you are still not ready. You are still worldly. For since there is jealousy and quarreling among you, are you not worldly? Are you not acting like mere men?"

The people to whom Paul was writing were Christians because Christ was in them, but they were not in the proper relationship with Him. They were not controlled by the mind of Christ, but by their own minds.

It is possible for someone to be a Christian for decades, having filled many offices in the church, and still be a "baby Christian." The world often looks at those inside the church acting like babies and sees them quarreling, fighting, bickering and disagreeing disagreeably. The world says, "If that's Christianity, I don't want anything to do with it. They're hypocrites!"

Such persons are called "carnal" in the *KJV* and persons "of the flesh" in the *RSV*. Flesh or self-centeredness is controlling their lives rather than Jesus Christ, and so there is conflict and struggle.

We all act like persons of the flesh from time to time. I was at a staff retreat recently, having just returned from my vacation. It was the type of vacation which leaves you more tired than when you left. I was frazzled. A situation occurred at the retreat in which I disagreed with two staff members, so I decided to exert my authority and settle the matter. Later, the incident continued to bother me. As I thought about it, I realized that instead of discussing the issue adult-to-adult, I had spoken to my staff members as a parent would speak to small children.

The following day when we met, I read aloud Romans 7:15, 19 and 24: "I do not understand what I do. For what I want to do I do not do, but what I hate I do. . . . For what I do is not the good I want to do; no, the evil I do not want to do—this I keep on doing. . . . What a wretched man I am! Who will rescue me from this body of death?"

Of all the mistakes I fear, patronizing fellow staff members is one of the greatest. But like Paul, I sometimes do the things I hate. As I confessed my sin to my staff, I felt like Paul did—a wretched person, a wretched friend and a wretched pastor. Each staff member responded and forgave me, and we were reconciled. When we are honest with ourselves, we realize that self-centeredness is more a part of our lives than we care to admit.

Live by the Spirit

Without a doubt, it is a struggle to be a spiritual Christian, one who is constantly controlled by the mind of Christ. Paul graphically described this struggle in Galatians 5:16-25. These passages speak of a war between the carnal person and the spiritual person within each of us. But Paul concluded that when we allow the Holy Spirit to control our lives, He will overcome the tendency toward sin in our lives.

Winning the War. How do we win this battle? By trying harder? No! We must allow ourselves to be controlled by the Holy Spirit who releases the power of Christ in us. Then we are filled with the Spirit. The lordship of Jesus is revealed in our lives and we find ourselves doing those things that please God. This is not a matter of trying harder; it is a matter of trusting more. I am using the concepts of allowing Jesus to be Lord and being filled or controlled by the Holy Spirit interchangeably for they are indeed synonymous.

We can relate to the war Paul wrote about because it is a real part of our experience in daily living. Let me further explain and illustrate the conflict by looking again at the three kinds of persons we have discussed.

Imagine a woman driving down the road and seeing a hitchhiker. She thinks she recognizes the man because there is something familiar about him. But she had heard too many frightening stories about hitchhikers. Since she does not know the man personally she drives by him without stopping.

Many people see Christ Jesus this way. They have heard something about Him, but they don't know Him personally. They think, "I'm not going to invite this Christ into my life; I have too much to lose." These are the unspiritual persons.

Now imagine the same woman seeing a hitchhiker she recognizes. "Oh, that's my neighbor! His car must have broken down. I'll stop and give him a ride."

This type of reaction is similar to that of believers who know and trust Jesus enough to invite Him into their lives as Savior, but won't relate to Him as Lord. They desire to be in control; they want to be in the driver's seat. This is the carnal Christian.

Finally, imagine this woman seeing a hitchhiker whom she recognizes to be her father. "Oh my goodness, that's my dad!" She not only stops to let him in, but she slides over and allows her father to do the driving, pleased to go with him wherever he decides to go. This is the Spirit-filled Christian. The Holy Spirit is in control and the driving and direction are left to Him.

Changing Drivers. When we were in seminary, my wife Jennifer and I would drive a great distance to see our families during the holidays. We tried to make the trip as fast as we could, stopping only for necessities.

Every hour we routinely changed drivers—but without stopping the car! I would move the front seat back as far as it would go, put my left foot on the gas pedal and my left hand on the wheel and slide over to the passenger's side. At the same time, Jennifer would climb over me, put her left foot on the gas pedal under my foot, put her left hand on the wheel and slip into the driver's seat as I was sliding out. We then had a big '65 Ford Galaxy which gave us more room to manuever than cars have today, so we could make our switch without the speedometer dropping more than two miles per hour!

I do *not* recommend this procedure. Seminarians sometimes do crazy things! But it does illustrate how you and I can spiritually "switch drivers" in our Christian lives. Without missing a beat, we can go from Spirit-control to self-control many times during the day.

The spiritual driver switch happens to me all the time. I have a blessed time with the Lord when I get up for prayer and Bible study at 6:00 A.M. The Spirit seems so near that I want to sing hymns of joy. I head to the breakfast table at 7:00 A.M., kiss Jennifer and beam beneficently at my boys. But then Christopher knocks over his cereal, Nathan spills the orange juice, Joshua belches and Jennifer burns her finger on the toaster. I get up to help her and I trip over Woofie our dog. Immediately I am "burned up" and say some unkind words to my family and some downright nasty words to Woofie!

In just a few seconds I shift from Spirit-control to Ron-control. All of a sudden I am not at my best. You see, the old nature is still within me and it is constantly at war with my new nature.

Filled and Flowing. Here are two more ways to visualize the advantage and blessing of being a Spirit-filled, Spirit-controlled person. Imagine three tires sitting side by side. First, there is an unmounted tire with no air in it. It is like a natural person with no wind (Spirit) inside. Next, there is a flat tire. It might be punctured by broken glass or a nail, or it may simply have been driven too far without being refilled. That tire won't run well; in fact, you could ruin your wheel trying to drive on it. That's like a carnal Christian. Finally, there is a mounted, balanced tire filled with air. It is like the Spirit-filled Christian.

Have you checked your spiritual air-pressure lately?

Are there some sins or distractions that need to be
removed from your life like nails from a flat tire? Do you
need to be renewed and refilled with the Spirit so you can
be everything that God created you to be?

Think about three faucets. The first faucet has no
water in it. Its pipe isn't connected to the water source.

> *In relational evangelism one first seeks to
> relate to another person—finds common
> ground or earns the right to be heard—and
> then looks for an opportunity to share the
> good news.*

That's a natural person. The next faucet is connected and
the water is running, but a build-up of sediment inside the
pipe clogs the flow. Any water that does get through is
dark and rusty. That's the carnal Christian. The old self
impedes and distorts the working of the Holy Spirit until
very little of Jesus Christ can be seen in the carnal Christian's life.

The third faucet has the living water flowing freely
through it. That's the spiritual person. Jesus said, "'Whoever believes in me, as the Scripture has said, streams of
living water will flow from within him.' By this he meant
the Spirit" (John 7:38,39). May this describe each of us as
we allow the Holy Spirit to fill us and control us to the
glory of God.

Seven Levels of Revealing The Good News

Throughout my years of equipping others in evangelism, I
have observed seven basic levels at which people reveal

their faith to others. I often compare these levels to different persons at the seashore.

First, there are persons who wade into the water about ankle deep and go no further. I call this "shallow evangelism." It describes those who use such phrases as "May God bless you," "The Lord be with you," "I'll pray about that," "Praise the Lord" and "The Man Upstairs was watching over me." These people simply try to bring God or some aspect about Him into a conversation.

Shallow evangelism also includes wearing religious jewelry, such as a cross, a fish, a dove or a lapel pin which says "Jesus First" or "One Way." Another form of shallow evangelism could be saying grace at a restaurant where others might be watching.

Second, there are persons who wade in and splash a little water on themselves without going in any deeper. I call this "relational evangelism." Paul exemplified this form of evangelism: "To the Jews I became like a Jew, to win the Jews. To those under the law I became like one under the law . . . so as to win those under the law. To those not having the law I became like one not having the law . . . so as to win those not having the law. To the weak I became weak, to win the weak. I have become all things to all men so that by all possible means I might have some" (1 Cor. 9:20-22).

In relational evangelism one first seeks to relate to another person—finds common ground or earns the right to be heard—and then looks for an opportunity to share the good news.

The third level of evangelism is like persons who jump right into the water by initiating a spiritual conversation. I call this "active evangelism."

A biblical example of active evangelism is the story of Jesus and the woman at the well in John 4. Jesus took the initiative, engaged the woman in casual and then spiritual conversation and announced that He was the Christ. In response to her encounter with Jesus, the Samaritan woman became the greatest evangelist in the Gospels. She was used by God to convert almost an entire city.

The fourth level of evangelism is illustrated by people at the beach who are thrown into the water by others. I

The persons who find themselves divinely appointed to share their faith are far beyond human circumstances or coincidences. These appointments are specially arranged by the Holy Spirit.

call this "passive evangelism" because others initiate a spiritual conversation and bring the Christian into it.

Jesus and Nicodemus exemplify passive evangelism in John 3. Nicodemus was aware of Jesus' life-style. He came to Jesus at night confessing that he knew Jesus was a man of God because of His miraculous works. It was then that Jesus opened His lips and revealed the plan of salvation to Nicodemus and invited him to be born again. At times people will come to you and begin a spiritual conversation. When this happens you don't need to search for common ground. They have already pulled you into the witnessing waters. Be prepared!

The fifth type of beach-goer is the one whose only purpose is to swim out into deep waters. This is the person who presents a clear plan of salvation to others, intending to lead them into a relationship with Christ. I call this "purpose evangelism." These witnesses prefer to cut through all the surface levels of evangelism and get right to the heart of sharing Christ.

Sixth, there are people who go to the seashore prepared for anything. They bring towels, umbrellas for sun or rain, suntan lotion, lunches, Thermos bottles and sunglasses. I call this "prepared evangelism" or "Boy Scout evangelism" because of the Scout's pledge to "be prepared."

These people reflect the words of Peter: "Always be prepared to give an answer to everyone who asks you to give the reason for the hope that you have. But do this with gentleness and respect" (1 Peter 3:15,16). Like the lifeguard on duty, a Christian on duty must be prepared at all times.

The seventh level of evangelism involves persons who walk out on the waters of witnessing in "divine appointment evangelism." These people find themselves in witnessing situations that are unexpected and divinely arranged. Peter was called by Christ to walk on water, something the disciple had not arranged. The persons who find themselves divinely appointed to share their faith are far beyond human circumstances or coincidences. These appointments are specially arranged by the Holy Spirit.

Many times the Spirit leads us to a divine appointment as He led Philip to the Ethiopian eunuch in Acts 8. Those who "walk on water" are in the right place at the right time. One of the keys to such appointments is to *be available* for God's use at any time. When we are available, He supplies the ability to minister in divinely appointed situations.

Reaching for Goals

When revealing the good news at any of these seven levels, there are several goals we should seek to reach.

Before sharing Jesus with our friends, one of our goals should be to create a favorable appetite for the good news in others so that they will desire to "taste and see that the LORD is good" (Ps. 34:8). We create this appetite by being pleasant in our approach and appearance, and positive in our presentation, for we are "the aroma of Christ" (2 Cor. 2:15).

Our purpose in sharing the good news should never be to force or argue a friend into making a commitment to Jesus Christ. Witnessing is not "winning." We are not engaged in a contest with an adversary, but a relationship with a friend.

During the sharing itself, our goal is to be sensitive to each individual and each individual situation. Paul exhorted: "Whether you eat or drink or whatever you do, do it all for the glory of God. Do not cause anyone to stumble . . . even as I try to please everybody in every way. For I am not seeking my own good but the good of many, so that they may be saved" (1 Cor. 10:31-33). Remember that people generally don't like to be surprised or cornered and "stung" by an insensitive witness.

Sensitivity is also expressed through variety. It is best if the person sharing the good news is acquainted with a variety of approaches. A person so equipped can choose the most appropriate methods to use with a particular person in a particular situation. Variety allows choice and choice conveys sensitivity. The many methods presented in this book will equip you to deal with many different persons and situations.

Following the sharing, your goal should always be to

leave your friend with such a favorable attitude that the opportunity to hear the gospel again from someone else will be welcomed. Our purpose in sharing the good news should never be to force or argue a friend into making a commitment to Jesus Christ. Witnessing is not "winning." We are not engaged in a contest with an adversary, but a relationship with a friend.

Understanding the three types of persons and the seven levels of revealing the good news serves as a basis for all the different approaches in FRIENDS evangelism. This foundation also equips us to understand ourselves, others and our ministry. What is our ministry? It is the ministry of revealing the good news through life and lips—by the power of the Holy Spirit—to those who have not yet responded to God's invitation in Jesus Christ. nd our ministry is also to those who have responded to Christ but who need to renew the enabling power of the Holy Spirit in their lives and become all that Christ created them to be.

CHAPTER 4
The ABCs of Christianity

And when I came to you, brethren, I did not come with superiority of speech or of wisdom, proclaiming to you the testimony of God. For I determined to know nothing among you except Jesus Christ, and Him crucified. 1 Corinthians 2:1,2, *NASB*

In 1962, while attending the University of North Dakota, I met a pretty young woman named Jennifer. We became fond of each other and often played the college game of "kissy face" while seated on the park bench.

One day Jennifer revealed to me some particular concerns in her life and asked for my advice. I pulled a New Testament out of my pocket and shared with her several passages which shed some light on a possible solution to her concerns. She was intrigued and wanted to know more about Jesus Christ and what it meant to believe in Him. After four hours of discussion, she expressed an interest in putting her personal trust in Jesus as her Savior and Lord. She acted on her desire by praying to receive Christ.

If I knew then what I know now about expressing my faith verbally, I could have presented a basic outline of salvation, with the same results, in about four minutes instead of four hours. We could have enjoyed three hours and 56 minutes more of "kissy face"! Now that's practical theology!

> *Being a friend wins you the right to be heard. But just being a friend is not enough. When the Holy Spirit presents the opportunity you must be ready to explain the basics of salvation and the Christian faith.*

Simplicity—A Key to Success

Right in the middle of the FRIENDS evangelism strategy is the specific activity of expressing your faith to your friends. Being a friend wins you the right to be heard. But just being a friend is not enough. When the Holy Spirit presents the opportunity you must be ready to explain the basics of salvation and the Christian faith.

When it comes to sharing our faith with others, my motto is KISS—*K*eep *I*t *S*hort and *S*imple. My own experience confirms that the most effective evangelistic approaches contain the following KISS features:

- They are brief and can be easily learned and taught to others.
- They are flexible and offer a variety of methods from which to choose, allowing sensitivity to particular needs and situations.
- They can be easily introduced into a friendly

conversation with any number of persons.
- They use a positive approach to people, particularly at the opening.
- They are Christ-centered rather than church- or denomination-centered.
- They use the Bible as a visual aid and a tool to bring the listener into direct contact with the Holy Spirit.
- They use repetition as a means of retention.
- They clearly present the gospel, the claims of Christ and the meaning of biblical faith.
- They recognize and deal with the needs of Christians who are living defeated lives instead of abundant lives.
- They include an invitation to commit, renew or rededicate one's life to Christ.

I believe that Christians need to be prepared to share the gospel at all times and to do so in ways which are clear, simple and easy to understand. The ABCs of Christianity method which is described in this chapter fits this description perfectly. This method proves that I am a bona fide graduate of the KISS school of theology!

There Must Be an Easier Way

In my first parish in Mora, Minnesota, six of our lay people expressed a desire to learn how to share their faith with their neighbors and friends. Two retired men, Vernon and Wes, were long- standing church members. Eva had been a Sunday School teacher for many years. And John, Wendy and Rita were from the youth group.

The seven of us traveled together to Minneapolis to

attend some evangelism seminars and we deligently studied the methods which were presented. John, Wendy and
Rita learned quickly. They worked with the rest of us,

> *Every person who has a personal relation-*
> *ship with Jesus Christ can learn to be an*
> *effective witness, especially to his or her*
> *friends.*

drilling us on the verses, questions and quotations which
were designed to lead a person to make a faith commitment to Jesus Christ.

Vernon was determined to learn despite what he called
his "sheet-rock skull." He took a tape recorder to bed with
him, put the speaker under his pillow and went to sleep
with the Bible verses softly playing over and over in his
ear. We called the exercise "Vernon's subconscious evangelism method."

But even with this innovation, the witnessing plan
didn't sink in for Vernon. The rest of us were also struggling with the amount of material to be learned and we
soon became discouraged. Wes summarized our frustration by saying, "No wonder people leave evangelism to the
clergy. There must be an easier way to learn how to share
the good news!"

I am convinced that most lay people have been condi-
tioned to think that evangelism is the sole responsibility of
the professional preachers. But that is not the example we
find in the New Testament. As discussed in chapter 2,
some Christians are specifically gifted in evangelism. But
every person who has a personal relationship with Jesus
Christ can learn to be an effective witness, especially to
his or her friends.

In the weeks which followed our discouraging experience, we developed our own simple method for sharing the gospel—the ABCs of Christianity. I use various parts of the ABCs approach at some point in almost all of my presentations of the gospel. I once used the ABCs as an outline for a sermon that ended with an opportunity for my listeners to make a decision for Christ. Many times in personal witnessing I write the 26 letters of the alphabet on a sheet of paper or napkin and match each letter to key words and verses which tell the story of salvation.

Give Your Friend a Hand

There are many ways to use the ABCs in witnessing, but one of the most effective involves using your hand as a visual aid. I have often shared the ABCs by writing the letters on my hand or a glove. Using your hand with the ABCs is a "handy" method because you carry your visual aid with you at all times (see illustration on next page).

1. Palm: The Introduction. We begin the ABCs on the open palm, just as we open our palms to shake hands when being introduced to someone.

The key words for this step are **A**—*All,* **B**—*Believe* and **C**—*Christ.* The Bible says that God loves *all* the people of the world. He proved His love by sending His Son *Christ* Jesus into the world to redeem us *all.* The Bible also says that *all* of us must *believe* in *Christ* Jesus as our personal Savior. In so doing we receive eternal life (see John 3:16).

2. Thumb: The Nature of Eternal Life. The key words for step 2 are **D**—*Deserve* and *Death,* **E**—*Earn,*

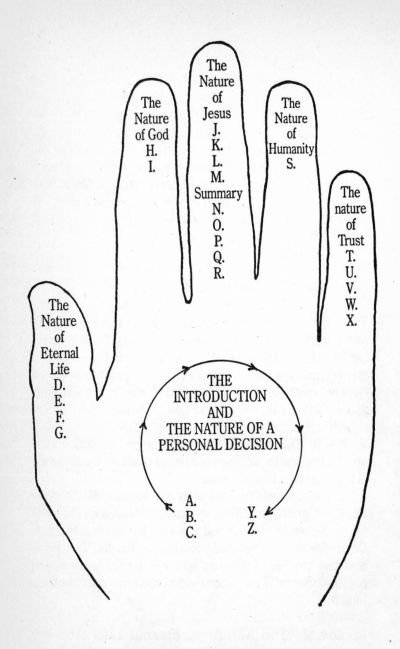

The
Nature
of
Jesus
J.
K.
L.
M.
Summary
N.
O.
P.
Q.
R.

The
Nature
of God
H.
I.

The
Nature
of
Humanity
S.

The
nature
of
Trust
T.
U.
V.
W.
X.

The
Nature
of
Eternal
Life
D.
E.
F.
G.

THE
INTRODUCTION
AND
THE NATURE OF A
PERSONAL DECISION

A.
B.
C.

Y.
Z.

F—*Free* and **G**—*God's Gift* of *Grace*. Eternal life, being with God forever, is something that we do not *deserve*, nor can we *earn* it. This is because we have a sinful nature. We *deserve death*, not life. Eternal life is a *free gift* of *God's grace* in Christ Jesus (see Rom. 6:23; Eph. 2:8,9). *Grace* is succinctly defined in the acronymn: *G*od's *R*edemption *A*t *C*hrist's *E*xpense.

3. First Finger: The Nature of God. The first finger is our "pointer" and also indicates "one way." Use it to point toward heaven as you talk about God's one way of salvation.

The key words for step 3 are **H**—*Holy* and **I**—*Initiative* and *Incarnation*. God is *holy*; He is without sin. We cannot fully comprehend this concept. God is *holy* and He calls us to be *holy* as He is *holy* (see 1 Pet. 1:15,16).

In order for us to become *holy*, God took the *initiative*. He became *incarnate* in Jesus Christ, which means He became flesh like us (see John 1:1,14; Rom. 5:8).

4. Middle Finger: The Nature of Jesus. The middle finger reminds us that Jesus stands in the middle. He is our mediator. He bridges the gap between sinful humanity and a holy God (see 1 Tim. 2:5).

The key words for step 4 are **J**—*Jesus*, **K**—*Kindness*, **L**—Love and **M**—*Mercy* and *Mankind*.

The name Jesus in Hebrew (*Yeshua*) and Greek (*Iasous*) means "He will save." In the Christmas story, Joseph was told to name Mary's baby *Jesus* "because He will save his people from their sins" (Matt. 1:21). The Bible says that we deserve and have earned judgment. But in *Jesus*, God reveals His *kindness*, His *love* and His *mercy* toward all *mankind* (see Neh. 9:17; Eph. 2:8,9).

The *M* also represents five things which pertain to

Jesus: He was born of the virgin *Mary* (see Luke 1:31); He became a *man* (see John 1:14); He became the *mediator* between God and mankind (see 1 Tim. 2:5); His death on the cross was God's *method* of salvation (see Matt. 16:21); and He is the only *means* of salvation (see John 14:6).

At this midpoint in the alphabet it is good to review the first four steps by repeating the key statements for *A* through *M*. Then add the following summary statement using the next five letters of the alphabet: There is N—*no* O—*other* P—*plan* Q—*quite* as R—*reliable* (see Acts 4:12; Heb. 9:22).

5. Ring Finger: The Nature of Humanity. The key words for step 5 are S—*Sheep, Sinful, Separated, Save, Savior* and *Shepherd.* The Bible compares us to *sheep* that have gone astray, each pursuing his own self-centered way (see Isa. 53:6).

We are *sinful* and therefore we are *separated* from our holy God. We cannot *save* ourselves. We need a *Savior* and *Shepherd* to lead us to God (see John 10:11).

6. Little Finger: The Nature of Trust. The key words for step 6 are T—*Total Trust,* U—*Universal,* V—*Verse,* W—*Whoever* and X—*Christ* (In Greek, *Christos* begins with the Greek letter *X*). We must *totally trust* Jesus, and Him alone, as our personal Savior (see Prov. 3:5). *Total trust* is the *universal* answer for all the people of the world (see 1 Tim. 2:3-6, especially in *The Living Bible*).

Perhaps the most familiar *verse* in the Bible says: "For God so loved the world that he gave his one and only Son, that *whoever* believes in him shall not perish but have eternal life" (John 3:16, italics added).

In John 11:26,27 we read: "'*Whoever* lives and believes

in me will never die. Do you believe this?'

"'Yes, Lord,' she told him, 'I believe that you are the *Christ'*" (italics added).

And the apostle John wrote: *"Whoever* believes that Jesus is the *Christ* is born of God" (1 John 5:1, *NASB*, italics added).

7. Palm: The Nature of a Personal Decision. We return to the palm for the final key words: **Y**—*You* and **Z**—*Zeal.* Do these verses (John 3:16; 11:26,27; 1 John 5:1) describe *you?* Have *you* ever with *zeal* (sincere meaning) prayed a prayer of salvation? It's as simple as ABC: Jesus, I *acknowledge* that I need you as my Savior (see Rom. 10:10). I *believe* in you and your work of salvation (see John 3:16). I *commit* my life to you (see Ps. 37:5; Rom. 12:1).

Two Important Techniques

The various methods of FRIENDS evangelism, including the ABC's, use two basic techniques. One is the Read and Review technique, and the other is the Direct Question/ Logical Answer technique.

The Read and Review technique is self-defining. Scripture passages are read and reviewed by you and your friend. The value of reading and reviewing each passage is that your friend better comprehends the content of the gospel message through repetition.

In the Direct Question/Logical Answer technique, specific questions are asked directly from the Scripture, leading to logical scriptural answers. The six journalistic questions of who, what, where, when, why and how are used to preface the direct questions. For example, you can use direct question and logical answer when sharing John 3:16 in the first step of the ABCs method: "For God so loved the world that he gave his one and only Son, that whoever believes in him shall not perish but have eternal life."

> Direct question: "For God so loved *what?*"
> Logical answer: "The world."
> Direct question: "For God so loved the world that He sent *whom?*" Logical answer: "His only Son."
> Direct question: "For God so loved the world that He sent His one and only Son, that whoever believes in Him shall not *what?*"
> Logical answer: "Shall not perish."

As shown, it is best to incorporate as much of the verse as possible into the question so that only the desired logical answer remains.

This is a valuable technique because the gospel message is taught logically, systematically and repetitiously. This technique is also highly personal and involves your friend directly with the *content* and *context* of the Scripture.

Clear and Simple

We were in the First Presbyterian Church in Huntington, West Virginia, teaching a variety of methods for sharing the good news. I had just concluded the Saturday morning session explaining the ABCs and the group was taking a break. I went into the kitchen and there was a cook who was wearing plastic gloves to mix macaroni salad.

"It's interesting that you're using those plastic gloves," I said to the cook. "Our group has just been discussing a method for sharing the gospel by using the fingers of our hands to remember our key points."

I asked her if she would like to hear some of the presentation. She agreed, so I held out my hand and went over the gospel using the ABCs.

I didn't think much about the incident until Sunday afternoon when I came into the kitchen to thank the kitchen crew for their ministry to our seminar. The cook I had spoken to introduced me to her daughter, the Sunday School superintendent at the church.

"Mom used her plastic glove to explain to me the ABCs of the gospel that you taught her yesterday," she said excitedly. "It was fascinating! This morning I called my teachers together before Sunday School, gave them plastic gloves and taught them your method. I suggested that they use the ABCs in their classes."

I was amazed. "Now let me get this straight," I said. "You didn't attend my seminar. You just heard about the ABCs from your mom because I shared with her in the kitchen yesterday?"

"That's right," she answered with a big grin.

"And from that second-hand lesson you taught the ABCs to your staff of teachers before classes this morning?"

"Absolutely!" she giggled. "And that's not all. Several of our children decided to make professions of faith after hearing the ABCs. I can't tell you how pleased I am. I'm planning to make the ABCs a regular feature of our Sunday School and our summer Bible School!"

What a great harvest from such a simple seed!

If He Can Do It, So Can I!

"*A, B, C—All* who *believe* in *Christ* will receive eternal life," the speaker said in a clear voice. *"D, E, F, G*—We don't *deserve* it and we can't *earn* it, because it is a *free gift* of *God's grace."*

The person sharing the gospel at the HELPER seminar was not a clergy person or an elder of a church or a Sunday School teacher. It was our son Nathan, who was eight years old at the time. I have taught the ABCs to thousands of people, but my foremost students have been our three sons. On this occasion, Nathan was part of our teaching team and his task was to teach the ABCs method of evangelism at the seminar.

When I called Nathan up front and introduced him as the teacher of the next segment, there was a good bit of laughter. People thought it was a joke to ask a child to teach all these adults how to share their faith. But I sat down and Nathan began reciting the alphabet as a gospel outline.

The classroom became very quiet and the people leaned forward to catch every word. Nathan went straight through the alphabet, and by the time he reached *X, Y* and *Z* he had explained the complete plan of salvation through Jesus Christ. He stopped and smiled, and everyone applauded. Then he took a big breath and said, "Now I'll go through the ABCs again and this time you repeat after me."

After Nathan's presentation several individuals came up to talk with both of us. One by one they confessed that they had been very reluctant to share their faith in the past. But after they heard Nathan communicate so effectively they admitted, "If a child can do it, so can I."

Christopher, our youngest son, shares his faith through magic tricks. When he was six years old, Chris went with me to Oklahoma City to help teach a HELPER seminar to several hundred Methodists, including the bishop. Chris used a simple slight-of-hand demonstration to present the gospel. The people were amused and impressed that a child could understand and share the message in an entertaining way. They realized that if a child could learn to communicate the gospel effectively with his friends, there was hope for adults.

When the Cabbage Patch Doll craze was sweeping the country, I thought our family would escape the mania since we have three rough-and-tough boys. But Jennifer and I underestimated the effectiveness of our nonsexist parenting. Nathan, who was nine years old then, just *had* to have a Cabbage Patch boy. I told him that if he wanted to be an adoptive parent, he had to be responsible for his own child. He must pay for the adoption out of his own savings. Nathan had no problem with my requirement; he did it gladly.

I'll never forget the night Nathan received his Cabbage Patch son, Whitney Rodrick Rand. He was so happy as he dressed Whitney in a fresh diaper and little pajamas, and settled down with him in his bedroom.

The next morning I overheard six-year-old Christopher tell Nathan, "Nate, you need to find out if Whitney knows the Lord."

"Nope," Nate replied. "He already does. I shared the ABCs of the gospel with him last night and he prayed to receive Jesus into his heart."

As they say, the apples don't fall far from the tree.

Faith Comes by Hearing

We once presented a HELPER seminar in a small town in Pennsylvania and several pastors were among our participants. Rev. Hal learned our ABCs and decided to use them in his radio sermon the following Sunday morning. At the opening of the broadcast, Rev. Hal asked his listeners to get paper and pencil during the singing of the hymn. He then instructed them to write out the alphabet and proceeded through the ABCs of Christianity, concluding with an invitation for people to commit their lives to Jesus Christ. Then he asked those who received Christ to drop a letter in the mail to tell him of their commitment and to receive follow-up literature.

To his amazement, Rev. Hal received more letters and phone calls after that broadcast than ever before! He was almost embarrassed as he heard the comment repeated, "Your ABC message was clearer than any you have preached before. At last you gave a simple outline of the gospel that I can understand!"

People Are Hungry to Hear

Doc, a member of our church and a good friend of mine, invited me to have lunch with him at an exclusive club in downtown Cincinnati. Doc met me at the door and we walked to an inner room where several men were seated around a table. As I sat down, Doc introduced the other men. An older gentleman on my right was the vice-president of a steel firm. Across from me were three justices in the Ohio supreme court. The fifth man, Joe, was a lawyer. Doc owns a large business himself. I felt a little out of my league at that table!

After the seven of us exchanged some stories and jokes, Joe said, "Ron, since you're a preacher, I've got a question for you. In fact," he rubbed his chin and smiled with a twinkle in his eye, "I've asked this question of several priests, rabbis and preachers."

"All right," I said, mentally preparing my theology. "Shoot."

"It's just a simple question," said Joe. "Who is God?"

A simple question, I thought as I stalled for time, wishing I could excuse myself and find a rear exit. I took a deep breath, smiled confidently (I hoped) and said, "That's an interesting question. I'm sure you've heard a variety of interesting answers. I'd like to answer you from what I understand the Bible to say about God.

"The Bible speaks about God as a loving heavenly Father who loved us to such an extent that He sent His only Son Jesus Christ into the world. Let me summarize the message of Christ by using the alphabet. Do you have some paper I can use?"

Joe reached into his coat pocket and pulled out a business envelope and his pen. On the back of the envelope I wrote the letters *A, B* and *C.* "The Bible can be summarized in one verse," I began.

"You probably know the verse—John 3:16. It says that all who believe in Jesus Christ have the gift of eternal life. ABC stands for *all* who *believe* in *Christ.* Now the next obvious question is what is eternal life?"

For the next several minutes I shared God's plan of salvation with Joe using the ABCs as an outline and guide. When I came to *Y* and *Z* I asked, "Joe, have *you* ever, with real *zeal*, asked Jesus to be your Savior and Lord?" Right there at the table, as the other businessmen watched and listened, Joe prayed aloud asking Jesus to forgive his sins and change his life. I'm not certain, but I suspect that was the first time anybody was born again in that club.

I pray that the ABCs method will become a natural part of your vocabulary. I hope you will delight in saying your ABCs to your friends and teaching them to do so to their friends.

CHAPTER 5

The Romans Invitation

*Now we rejoice in our wonderful new
relationship with God—all because of what
our Lord Jesus Christ has done in dying for
our sins—making us friends of God.*
Romans 5:11, *TLB*

Don is a captain in the Cincinnati Police Department and a
member of our church. He is rugged and tough—my idea
of a "macho" guy. To complete the image, Don rides a
huge black motorcycle—the kind that rattles the dishes in
the cabinet when the bike roars by.

Don befriended a young man in his neighborhood, an
energetic freshman at the University of Cincinnati named
Troy Coleman. Troy also had a motorcycle, but he couldn't
seem to get it to run the way he thought it should. So
Troy's cycle was scattered in pieces on the driveway more
often than it was together, much to the dismay of the Coleman family.

Don offered to help Troy work on his bike. Troy
accepted Don's persistent offer of assistance and advice
because he admired Don's bike (F—*Find* common
ground). While helping Troy put the broken motorcycle
together, Don took the opportunity to ask about the
church Troy's family attended. Was the church meaningful

to Troy? Who did he understand Jesus Christ to be? What did Christmas and Easter mean to him?

Don explained that he wouldn't come over to work on the motorcycle on Sundays because he would be at church (**R**—*Reveal* your faith through your life). Soon Troy was attending church with Don and asking many questions about God and Jesus Christ. Don also added Troy to his prayer list (**I**—*Intercede* for your friend).

Since Don is a member of our church, he has been trained in FRIENDS evangelism methods. When the opportunity presented itself, Don used one of these methods—called the Romans Invitation—to explain to Troy how God invites each of us into a personal relationship with Him through Jesus Christ (**E**—*Express* your faith through your lips). Troy prayed to receive Christ, and Don immediately went to work discipling his young friend in an understanding of the Scriptures and the ways of following Jesus Christ (**N**—*Nurture* and **D**—*Disciple* your friend to follow Jesus).

Troy eventually became a member of our church and he was also trained in the FRIENDS evangelism methods for sharing his new faith. He particularly wanted to apply what he learned to his family. It was through Troy that his dad, mom and two brothers—Clyde, Betty, Scott and Andy—came to know Christ as their personal Savior (**S**—*Set* your friends on a FRIENDS course). Clyde and Betty joined the church and, a short time later, brought their grown daughter Phyllis into the family of faith.

The *Oikos* Factor

The story of Don, Troy and the Coleman family is a perfect example of *oikos*, or household evangelism (based on

the Greek word for household). *Oikos* identifies your
existing relationships. Your *oikos* consists of your family,
friends and associates—those with whom you have
already won the right to be heard. Don reached out to his
friend Troy through the common interest of motorcycles.
Troy in turn reached out to his parents. Then his parents
reached out to more members of the household. See how
the circle of influence expands outwardly?

*I have seen persons who were so amazed
at the simplicity of the gospel when they
heard it in familar words that they immediately opened their hearts to Jesus Christ.*

Remember: Some people come to a church because it
is conveniently located; a few come because they feel a
special need in their lives; and a handful come because of a
decision made at some evangelistic crusade. But over 90
percent of church members began attending because
some member of their family or a close friend cared about
them and invited them to come. That's *oikos*! That's
FRIENDS evangelism!

Issuing the Romans Invitation

As with Don, Troy and his parents, your *oikos* relationships will eventually afford you the opportunity to talk to
your friends about God. The Romans Invitation method of
evangelism is ideally suited to *oikos* because it is simple,
clear and easily adaptable to any situation.

The Romans Invitation is designed to clearly reveal the
gospel using only the book of Romans. This approach has

become one of the most popular methods of witnessing used by our church members because it eliminates a lot of flipping back and forth, hunting for scattered Bible passages.

The basis of this approach is God's invitation of love through Jesus Christ to all humankind. It uses linear logic in that it establishes one point in a particular passage which leads naturally to another point and passage, and so on until a conclusion is reached. The technique of reading and reviewing each passage of Scripture, as described in chapter 4, allows for better understanding and greater clarity.

This approach is also very effective with an individual who is already a Christian. It builds a foundation for considering the need for renewal or rededication of one's life, or an area of one's life, to the control of Jesus Christ. The Christian's struggle between the flesh and the Spirit is examined in Romans 7 and 8.

It is very helpful for witnesses to be familiar with a variety of different translations and versions of Scripture, especially the popular modern language versions. The Romans Invitation is based on passages from Romans in *The Living Bible*. I have often used *The Greatest Is Love* edition of the New Testament (*TLB*) because it is inexpensive and easily understood. I have also found the pictures included in its pages to be very useful in witnessing at times.

A great advantage of *The Living Bible* is that it makes the content of Scripture accessible to people today, regardless of their level of education or exposure to traditional Christianity. Sadly, some persons feel that the Bible is mysterious and impossible to understand. It may be that they get this impression from hearing Scriptures read in archaic English. I have seen persons who were so amazed at the simplicity of the gospel when they heard it in familar words that they immediately opened their hearts to Jesus Christ.

If another reliable translation, version or paraphrase of the Bible is preferred, it may be substituted and used just as effectively with this approach. The Romans Invitation gets its name from the theme of invitation in the *The Living Bible* version of Romans. I have also developed a second version, called the Romans Reconciliation, which is based on the theme of reconciliation as found in the *New International Version*, the *Revised Standard Version*, the *New American Standard Bible* and the *King James Version*. First we will examine and illustrate the Romans Invitation. Then we will show how to adapt the Romans Invitation to other Bible versions with the Romans Reconciliation.

In this outline and example, we will call the friend who is sharing the gospel Bob. Bob's friend, who is interested in hearing the good news, we'll call Dave. Bob encourages Dave to read each passage out loud. Then Bob reviews and summarizes each passage.

1. Introduction

Bob: Dave, I think we know one another well enough for me to be very open and honest with you. I'm sure that you've noticed that my faith in Jesus Christ is an important part of my life. And because I feel that we have a close relationship, I would like to share the meaning of this faith with you. Could we look together at one of the most amazing invitations in the New Testament?

2. The Invitation in Romans

Bob: Let's begin by reading Romans 1:16,17. Dave, would you read it out loud please?

Dave: "For I am not ashamed of this Good News about Christ. It is God's powerful method of bringing all who believe it to heaven. This message was preached first to the Jews alone, but now everyone is invited to come to God in this same way. This Good News tells us that God makes us ready for heaven—makes us right in God's sight—when we put our faith and trust in Christ to save us. This is accomplished from start to finish by faith" (*TLB*).

Bob: Dave, to summarize these verses, we note in verse 16 that everyone is invited to come to God. Verse 17 tells us that the invitation can be accepted through faith in Jesus Christ. This is an amazing invitation because of what we read in Romans 3:21-24.

Dave: "Now God has shown us a different way to heaven—not by 'being good enough' and trying to keep his laws, but by a new way . . . Now God says he will accept and acquit us—declare us 'not guilty'—if we trust Jesus Christ to take away our sins. And we all can be saved in this same way, by coming to Christ, no matter who we are or what we have been like. Yes, all have sinned; all fall short of God's glorious ideal; yet now God declares us 'not guilty'" (*TLB*).

Bob: Dave, we see in verse 22 that all people are invited to come to Christ, no matter who they are. And notice in verse 23 that all are invited to come, even though all are sinners. The reason for this amazing invitation is found in Romans 5:8.

Dave: "God showed his great love for us by sending Christ to die for us while we were still sinners" (*TLB*).

Bob: Dave, it is clear from verse 8 that God loves everyone, including you and me, even though everyone is sinful. The purpose of this amazing invitation is revealed in Romans 5:10,11.

Dave: "Since, when we were his enemies, we were brought back to God by the death of his Son, what blessings he must have for us now that we are his friends, and he is living within us! Now we rejoice in our wonderful new relationship with God—all because of what our Lord Jesus Christ has done in dying for our sins—making us friends of God" (*TLB*).

Bob: Finally, to summarize verse 11, we see that God wants to bring us into a wonderful relationship with Him through Jesus Christ. Christianity is a personal relationship religion.

3. The Comprehension Question

Bob: Have these verses been clear to you Dave?

(If Dave answers no, Bob reviews the passages from Romans 1, 3 and 5 again, or any specific questions Dave has.)

Dave: Yes, I think I understand what these verses are saying.

Bob: Romans 5:1,2 summarize what has been said so far. Will you read them for us Dave?

Dave: "So now, since we have been made right in God's sight by faith in his promises, we can have real peace with him because of what Jesus Christ our Lord has done for us. For because of our faith, he has brought us into this place of highest privilege where we now stand, and we confidently and joyfully look forward to actually becoming all that God has had in mind for us to be" (*TLB*).

Bob: According to verse 1, we have been made right in God's sight by faith. (If necessary, explain and illustrate faith using the stories and illustrations in the Appendix.)

4. The Clarifying Question

Bob: Dave, have you ever responded to God's invitation by putting your faith in Jesus Christ as your personal Savior? (If Dave answers no, Bob moves to the Commitment Question below.)

Dave: Yes I have.

Bob: That's wonderful! Would you mind sharing with me the circumstances of your personal faith?

(If Dave gives definite testimony of a prior commitment to Christ, Bob proceeds to the Renewal Approach, described in chapter 6. But if Dave's explanation causes Bob to doubt a valid commitment to Christ, he can discuss with Dave the meaning of a personal faith commitment. See the President Example and the Marriage Example, helpful illustrations of commitment, in the Appendix.)

5. The Commitment Question

Bob: Dave, when you think of what He has done for you, do you desire to put your faith in Jesus Christ as your personal Savior?

(If Dave answers no, Bob may sensitively seek to discover the reason or simply thank Dave for the opportunity to talk as friends.)

Dave: Yes, I want to have faith in Christ.

6. The Commitment Prayer

Bob: Dave, your faith commitment to Christ can be expressed in a simple ABC prayer: I *accept* your invitation. I *believe* in Jesus Christ for the forgiveness of my sins. I now *come* to Him through faith. (Dave encourages Bob to pray the prayer aloud, perhaps leading him phrase by phrase.)

7. Immediate Follow-up

Bob: Dave, let's look at Romans 5:2 and discover what

happened as a result of your prayer of faith. Will you read it again please?

Dave: "For because of our faith, he has brought us into this place of highest privilege where we now stand, and we confidently and joyfully look forward to actually becoming all that God has had in mind for us to be" (*TLB*).

(Bob assures Dave that this verse is now true of him as a result of his faith in Christ.)

Bob: Dave, my prayer for you is in Romans 15:13: "So I pray for you . . . that God who gives you hope will keep you happy and full of peace as you believe in him. I pray that God will help you overflow with hope in him through the Holy Spirit's power within you" (*TLB*).

The Romans Reconciliation

The Romans Reconciliation approach uses the same passages and follows the same outline as the Romans Invitation. In fact, five of the seven steps—(1) Introduction, (3) Comprehension Question, (5) Commitment Question, (6) Commitment Prayer and (7) Immediate Follow-up—are identical. The differences in the presentation—(2) Romans passages and (4) Clarifying Question—reflect the theme of reconciliation which is more evident in other Bible versions than in *The Living Bible*.

In the example below, Sharon shares the gospel with Jan using the Romans Reconciliation approach and the *New International Version*. Imagine that Sharon has already completed an introduction similar to the example of Bob and Dave.

Reconciliation in Romans
Sharon: Let's begin by reading Romans 1:16,17. Jan, would you read it out loud please?

Jan: "I am not ashamed of the gospel, because it is the power of God for the salvation of everyone who believes: first for the Jew, then for the Gentile. For in the gospel a righteousness from God is revealed, a righteousness that is by faith from first to last, just as it is written: 'The righteous will live by faith.'"

Sharon: In summary Jan, verse 16 reveals that the power of God for salvation is for everyone. Verse 17 states that this salvation is available through faith in Jesus Christ. This is an amazing revelation because of what we read in Romans 3:21-24.

Jan: "But now a righteousness from God, apart from the law, has been made known, to which the Law and the Prophets testify. This righteousness from God comes through faith in Jesus Christ to all who believe. There is no difference, for all have sinned and fall short of the glory of God, and are justified freely by his grace through the redemption that came by Christ Jesus."

Sharon: Jan, verse 22 says that righteousness is offered to all people. And verse 23 affirms that all are eligible, even though all are sinners. The reason for this amazing revelation is explained in Romans 5:8.

Jan: "But God demonstrates his own love for us in this: While we were still sinners, Christ died for us."

Sharon: According to verse 8, Jan, God loves everyone, including you and me, even though everyone is sinful. The purpose of this amazing revelation is outlined Romans 5:10,11.

Jan: "If, when we were God's enemies, we were reconciled to him through the death of his Son, how much more, having been reconciled, shall we be saved through his life! Not only is this so, but we also rejoice in God through our Lord Jesus Christ, through whom we have now received reconciliation."

Sharon: Finally, to summarize these verses, we see that we are reconciled to God through the death of His Son and we are no longer enemies of God. If we are no longer enemies of God, and it is God Himself who desires to be reconciled to us, then we are in a joyful, loving relationship with God. Christianity is a personal relationship religion.

If your friend expresses firm unwillingness to hear more or to make a commitment to Christ, respect that position. The most important goal in this situation is to keep your relationship intact. Continue to be a friend and to reveal Christ's love through your life.

The Clarifying Question for Reconciliation

(After posing the Comprehension Question and dealing with Jan's response as in the example of Bob and Dave, Sharon asks the Clarifying Question based on the reconciliation theme.)

Sharon: Jan, have you ever responded to God's reconciliation by putting your faith in Jesus Christ as your personal Savior? (Sharon will proceed according to Jan's answer as in the previous example.)

No Full Court Press

It is difficult for me to emphasize in print how adamantly I feel *against* applying pressure in a witnessing presentation. We've all heard it said that Jesus is a gentleman who never enters where He is not invited. I believe it. You are not doing your friends a favor by pressuring them into saying the appropriate words just to get rid of you. If your friend expresses firm unwillingness to hear more or to make a commitment to Christ, respect that position. The most important goal in this situation is to keep your relationship intact. Continue to be a friend and to reveal Christ's love through your life.

Your friend may not be ready to make a commitment for one of the following reasons:

- "I'm not good enough to be a Christian."
- "I don't think I can live up to such a commitment."
- "I'm afraid I'll let Christ down if I make a commitment."
- "I don't really understand everything yet."
- "I understand what's been said, but I'm not ready to take that step."

These reasons often stem from sincerity, humility and intellectual honesty. Affirm that honesty and try to resolve the difficulty with sensitivity and respect. Scripture is the best resource for answering your friend's objections. Use the Romans passages and 1 John 1:8-10 to stress that everybody sins, but that we also seek to be forgiven and cleansed as we live for Christ.

If after further discussion your friend still feels reticent to make a commitment, you must respect and affirm that position. Your purpose for sharing the gospel should never be to force or argue a person into making a commitment to Christ. You want to leave your friend with such a favorable attitude that they will welcome the opportunity to hear the gospel again at a later time. If possible, give your friend a Bible or New Testament with the Romans passages clearly marked. Suggest that he or she also read the Gospel of John.

A Family Affair

When the children of our church members are baptized, many relatives, neighbors and friends attend the service to observe. The Johnsons invited their neighbor Herb to come witness the baptism of their child. As a result, Herb began asking them questions about their church and their faith. Herb grew up in a ritualistic church that did not encourage close involvement with the Scriptures. When David Johnson and Herb sat down over coffee, Herb had 101 questions about the Bible. He had such a hunger for the Scriptures!

David gave Herb a copy of the New Testament and the two neighbors met regularly in the evenings exploring the Bible to answer Herb's questions. Herb was amazed that the Bible had present-day answers for his present-day questions. There were times when David couldn't answer Herb's questions. But he always wrote them down and returned the next week with thoughts from the research he had done. David came to me with a few of Herb's questions, so I gave him some ideas and loaned him books to study. I also offered to accompany him and talk with Herb.

The next week David suggested the idea to Herb, who was delighted to invite me to his home. He said he could relate to me because he heard me preach once at College Hill Presbyterian Church. He felt good about being with a guy who could admit his mistakes and even laugh at himself in front of the whole congregation!

After six weeks of meeting with David and me, Herb was ready to put his faith in Jesus Christ. He had heard the Romans Invitation from David and he had explored and understood the Word himself. Whenever David visited in Herb's home, he noticed that Herb's son was in the dining room doing homework, overhearing the Bible discussions. When it came time for Herb to pray asking Jesus to be the Lord of his life, he told David that he and his boy had discussed the Bible together after David's visits. They had *both* decided to commit their lives to Jesus Christ. Herb asked David if the three of them could kneel together by the coffee table and light a candle. They did, and both Herb and his son confessed their sins and committed their lives to Jesus as their Savior and Lord.

Being a Good News Storyteller

When I was coaching baseball, there was one couple— Mark and Laurie Miller—experiencing problems in their marriage and in his employment. Their difficulties were reflected in the behavior and conversation of their son Timothy, one of my players, at practice. Mark and Laurie observed the way I encouraged Timothy and worked with his teammates. They liked what they saw and wanted to hear more. It wasn't long before they asked me to visit them at home.

When I called on the Millers, I brought our son Joshua, who was nine at the time. Mark and Laurie shared that their problems had been building during their 12-year marriage. Everything seemed to stem from their different religious backgrounds. Mark grew up in a formal, impersonal church and Laurie in a more participatory congregation.

Mark's pastor disapproved of his relationship with Laurie. He told them that their marriage would be condemned by his church and that any children they might have would be unclean in God's sight!

You can just imagine the shame and guilt this couple brought into their marriage. And after 12 years and three children, it seemed that their lives were falling apart in all directions. I thought of the woman who suffered for 12 years with a flow of blood that nobody could heal until she reached out to touch Jesus. It was as though Mark's pastor had brought a curse on them that they could not escape.

After listening carefully as the Millers vented their pain, Joshua and I offered them copies of the New Testament. We suggested that we look at the passages in the Romans Invitation, sensing that this method would minister to their needs. Joshua read the verses from the third chapter of Romans, revealing that it didn't make any difference who we were or what we had done or believed in the past. God said that He would acquit us and accept us if we would only put our faith in Jesus Christ.

If ever I have seen the Holy Spirit move upon anyone, He did so in that little living room on the Millers. They read the passages along with Joshua, and then they called in all their children to hear what seemed to be written by God especially for their family.

With the time getting late on a school night, we interrupted our conversation to get our children into bed. We lived only a few blocks away, so we excused ourselves and I hustled Joshua back to our house and into his pajamas. As I was about to kiss him good night and pray with him, Joshua seemed to glow with the Spirit.

"You know, Dad," he said, "I could really see a change in their faces when I read those verses. It made me feel really good."

"Joshua, that was the Holy Spirit you saw," I told him. "That's the greatest joy I know, and it's a great privilege to share the good news." We joyously prayed together, thanking God for using us as His good news storytellers.

I returned to the Miller's home and they were eager to continue the discussion. So I completed the passages in Romans and before the evening was over they knelt with me beside their couch to welcome Jesus Christ into their lives.

The Millers experienced a great healing and many blessings as they accepted God's forgiveness and discovered their freedom in Jesus Christ. I had earned the right to be heard through three years of encouragement and patience as Timothy's baseball coach. Through that friendship, Joshua and I were able to share with them, using the Romans Invitation, about a friendship with Jesus Christ.

An Invitation of Love

I am so thankful to the Lord for these verses in Romans revealing His love and His initiative in sharing His love through Jesus Christ. I find that I use these verses frequently in many different contexts when I witness to others. I have even used these verses as an outline when preaching to the masses of vacationing students gathered on the Florida beaches. It was a difficult and demanding experience to say the least. Yet the Romans Invitation verses provoked many listening students to consider the personal invitation from God to enter into a loving and forgiving personal relationship. I believe you will have the same experience as you share the Romans Invitation with your friends.

CHAPTER 6

The Renewal Approach

*Those who live according to the sinful
nature have their minds set on what that
nature desires; but those who live in
accordance with the Spirit have their
minds set on what the Spirit desires.*
Romans 8:5

One weekday morning I was driving our oldest son Joshua
to school. I was late for a staff meeting so I was rushing. I
glanced in the rear view mirror to see an emergency vehicle approaching. I dutifully pulled over to let it pass, but to
my surprise and chagrin, it didn't pass. A police car pulled
up behind me with the flashing blue bubble light advertis-
ing that a lawbreaker had been caught in the act! The
trooper got out, straightened his hat and strolled up to my
car. He informed me that I had been driving 40 mph in a 25
mph zone and wrote me a ticket.

In that small suburb of Cincinnati, you can't just accept
the ticket, conveniently write a check or money order and
mail it to the Justice Department. You must make a court
appearance. I decided that since Joshua had been with me
at the "scene of the crime," it would be appropriate and
instructional to take him with me to court. I wanted him to
know firsthand that there are always consequences for
breaking the law.

The courtroom was an informal set-up in the local fire station. All the people were seated in the back of the room, well apart from one another. No one was smiling. They all sat quietly with their heads bowed and their hands folded. I felt right at home because it was just like a Presbyterian church!

Then a person, who was kind of like an associate minister, came in and gave the call to worship in King James' English: "Hear ye, hear ye. The court is now in session. All please rise." Everyone stood up to show their respect to the judge who, like a senior pastor, entered dressed in a black clerical robe. But instead of carrying a Bible, the man held a gavel. When he sat, everybody sat. There was no hymn at that service!

Then the court seemed to change from a Presbyterian service to sort of a revival service. There was no piano playing "Just as I Am," but everyone responded to the altar call—each person repentantly walking forward to confess his or her sin before the judge.

Finally it was my turn and I walked up the aisle with Joshua. Without looking up, the judge asked, "How do you plead, Mr. Rand?"

I said, "Guilty, your honor."

The judge looked at me and saw six-year old Joshua trying to be invisible behind my legs. "Is this your son, Mr. Rand?" he asked.

"Yes, your honor. I brought him with me because he was with me at the scene of the crime. I wanted him to learn that there are always unpleasant consequences to breaking the law."

Without missing a beat, the judge said, "If that is the case, Mr. Rand, who is going to take your son home while you spend the night in jail?"

I was momentarily speechless. Then I noticed a twitch

at the corner of the judge's mouth. "Well, your honor, I also hoped that he would learn something about mercy."

Laughter broke out behind us in the courtroom. The judge announced my fine and I wrote my check, knowing that my penalty had been paid and justice had been served.

Who's in Charge?

I often relate this experience as an illustration of the difference between law and grace. I paid my fine, knowing that I deserved that penalty. It was justice. I did not go to jail because that would have been more punishment than I deserved. But I did not receive grace. The judge did not let me go home without paying the fine.

There is another lesson in my experience: the Reverend Dr. Ronald R. Rand does not always live the way Jesus Christ wants him to live. Sometimes I break the speed limit. And that's not all. Sometimes I shout in anger at my sons. Sometimes I neglect my wife. Sometimes I'm insensitive and self-centered and lazy.

What? Can I be a Christian and still behave like that, sometimes breaking the law and hurting persons who love me? Yes, I'm sorry to say, it's true more often than I like to admit. I am thoroughly Christian, but sometimes my behavior is thoroughly unchristian. And this is true of all Christians, as I learned early in my ministry.

In September of my second year at the church in Mora, I met with the six members of our board of elders to plan the worship services through Advent. I decided that it would be nice to have a candlelight service on Christmas Eve. You have probably attended such a service. The sanctuary lights are dimmed and the elders each light a candle from one large "Christ candle." Then they pass through the aisles lighting small candles held by members of the congregation until the entire church is filled with a lovely glow.

When I asked the elders to consider a candlelight service they promptly and emphatically said no. They reminded me that our new sanctuary had padded pews and a new carpet. They didn't want any burn spots or wax drippings on the wood or fabric. And there was a clause in our insurance policy that specified responsible use of candles. And finally, didn't I know that many of our members used hair spray, which is very flammable? Somebody's hair might catch on fire!

Wow! I just blew up! Here were the elders of the church putting more value on material things than on spiritual things. Were we trusting in our insurance policies or were we trusting in God? Were we more concerned about the beauty of furniture or the beauty of holiness? We left the meeting in a six-to-one standoff. I was determined to have my way, and they were just as determined to let me know who was in charge.

It was in this state of mind that I left for a two-day conference. I traveled with five other ministers to Minneapolis for a conference on spiritual renewal. I was the new kid on the block, fresh out of seminary. I had been in the community barely 18 months.

We arrived late for the conference. As we shuffled into an empty pew, two lay persons were already teaching from Romans, Galatians and 1 Corinthians about the three types of persons—spiritual, unspiritual and carnal. They drew some illustrations on the chalkboard describing the carnal Christian who does not allow Jesus Christ to be Lord in every area of life. This person, they said, was self-righteous, proud and competitive, always seeking his own way and wanting to be in charge. He would lose his love for others, lose his desire for Bible study and fail to find time for prayer.

What conviction! It was easy to admit that my prayer and Bible study had slipped. But it was difficult for me to admit that I wanted to be in charge at my church more than I wanted the Lord to be in charge of me. When the speakers closed the teaching session, they gave an opportunity for those who identified with the person they had described to pray silently. Then they asked those who felt the need to express their repentance in a physical way to stand up, indicating that they had asked the Holy Spirit to take control of their lives. I almost jumped to my feet. And when the prayer was over, I saw that almost every pastor in the sanctuary was standing. There was a lot of confession and reconciliation in the group that night. It was a very important time for me.

When I came back to Mora I called a special meeting of the elders and shared with them what I had learned. I asked for their forgiveness and said that whatever they wanted to do on Christmas Eve would be fine with me. Two of the elders must have thought they would never see me so meek again, so they took the opportunity to point out other areas that I needed to clean up. Thankfully, the Holy Spirit was with me. I was able to receive what they said without my blood pressure rising. I asked for their forgiveness for each offense. We all prayed together before they left.

Afterward I lingered in the office to pray about what to do next. As I was praying there was a knock at the door. Two of the elders came back in and asked, "What happened to you at that conference, Ron? Tell us more."

I shared with them more of what I learned at the conference. Then these two elders decided that they needed to be renewed in Jesus Christ also. They wanted to let the

Spirit be in charge of their words and actions. After that evening, things gradually changed in our church. It might have been appropriate to hang a sign on the door: New Manager in Charge.

Relationship and Renewal

Suppose I perform a wedding uniting Jack and Janet as man and wife. It is such a lovely service. Janet looks so pretty and Jack is so proud! They leave on their honeymoon and then come home to a cute little house with plans for starting a family.

But a week after the honeymoon Jack and Janet knock on my office door. "Something terrible has happened!" they tell me. "We had an awful fight and said nasty, unloving things to each other. Our relationship isn't right, so you need to marry us again."

What would you say if you were me? Do they need to have another wedding and recite new vows in order to restore a right relationship? Of course not! Jack and Janet are still married because they vowed, "Till death do us part." They don't need another wedding, but they do need to put into practice the "for better or worse" part. They need to be reconciled and renewed by admitting their faults and forgiving one another.

This is also true about our relationship with Jesus Christ. Even though we have a personal relationship with God through Jesus Christ, we all continue to sin. We frequently fail to live as God wants us to live. When sin fouls our relationship with God, we don't need to go back to the altar and receive Christ again. But we do need to approach Him with confession so the harmony of our relationship can be restored.

Sharing Renewal with Your Friends

Let's go back to the Romans Invitation and assume that your friend answered the Clarifying Question: "Yes, I have put my faith in Jesus Christ as my personal Savior."

"Friend, that's wonderful!" you respond. "We saw in Romans 5 that faith in Jesus Christ brings us into a new relationship with God. Would you mind sharing with me the circumstances that caused you to put your faith in Jesus Christ as your personal Savior?"

This question allows you to determine the extent of your friend's commitment to Christ. It may very well be that he or she really is a Christian, but do not assume this too quickly. Try to bring the validity of the commitment out into the open.

Do not be as concerned with the manner or method of encountering Christ as with the reality and sincerity of personal faith in Christ.

As you listen to your friend's testimony, make sure you don't judge the reality of his or her faith on the presence or absence of Christian jargon. It's possible to be a Christian without describing the relationship with such terms as born again, decision for Christ, saved, spiritual birthday, Jesus in my heart or a personal relationship with Jesus. Be open to each unique experience of encountering Christ.

On the other hand, your friends may talk about being saved because they have heard Christians using that phrase, but they may not have a personal relationship with Jesus Christ. Do not be as concerned with the manner or method of encountering Christ as with the reality and sincerity of personal faith in Christ.

> *We need to let Christ renew His control of our lives day by day and moment by moment, because that's how often we wrongly take control of our lives from Him.*

If your friend's testimony does not reveal a personal faith commitment to Christ, you will continue with the Romans Invitation as described in chapter 5. The following steps for renewal are based on your friend's affirmative response that he or she has made a personal commitment to Christ in the past.

1. Your Personal Testimony. Express your appreciation for your friend's willingness to share his or her testimony with you. Then briefly give your testimony of receiving Christ.

In preparation for looking into the renewal passages with your friend, say something like: "I would like to share with you something that has been meaningful to me since I became a Christian. It's how I've learned to let Christ be my Lord daily. Even though I have committed my life to Jesus Christ, I still continue to sin. This fact greatly disturbed me, and many times I wondered if I really was a Christian at all. Often I asked myself how I could be a Christian when I continued to do those things that were displeasing to Christ. Have you ever asked yourself that same question?"

If your friend is like most Christians, he or she will

admit occasional doubts and discouragement over personal sins.

2. The Need for Renewal. Direct your friend's attention to Romans 7:15-25, referring to the passage as your autobiography because it is a commentary which you could have written on your own life. Read—or have your friend read—verses 15-25 out loud. Then discuss the following main points found in verses 23-25:

　a. There are two natures present within the Christian. One is a new, Christ-centered nature and the other is an old, sinful, self-centered nature.

　b. These two natures are at war with each other within us. When Christ, through the Holy Spirit, is in control of our lives, we do things that please Him. When we are in control of our lives, we do things that may please us but displease God. We displease the Lord daily when we control our lives instead of letting the Holy Spirit control us. When we control our lives, Jesus is not allowed to be the Lord or authority of our lives. (You may want to give a personal example of a recent battle with sin. Your openness and honesty will help your friend be honest with himself or herself.)

　c. When Jesus is allowed to be Lord, He sets us free to be what He created us to be. The key to this freedom is discovering God's pathway to renewal.

3. The Path to Renewal. You may continue by saying, "I have discovered how to have victory in this war going on inside of me." Then read out loud with your friend Romans 8:4,5,9. Verse 9 is the key to calling for renewal.

Say something like: "It was most helpful when I discovered who I was allowing to control my life. It says in verse 9 that those who let themselves be controlled by themselves live only to please themselves. But those who let themselves be controlled by the Holy Spirit—that is, Christ—find themselves doing those things that please God.

"The key is to *allow* Christ to control my life. For then I will do those things that please Him. That is how to have victory in the war."

The word WAR is a helpful acrostic for allowing Christ be in control of our lives. We must honestly ask ourselves if we really *want* Christ to be in control of our lives. We must truthfully admit that there are times in our lives when we want to be in control instead of allowing Christ to be in control.

Realizing the opportunity of continually renewing Christ's lordship in our lives can make the difference between despair and hope in the life of an individual. Personal renewal can also make the difference between dreariness and excitement in the life of a congregation.

If we truly want Christ to be in control, we only need to *ask* Him to forgive us and take control again as Lord. We must further allow Him to *renew* His control of our lives as we turn from the wrong we were doing. We need to let Christ renew His control of our lives day by day and moment by moment, because that's how often we wrongly take control of our lives from Him.

3. The Comprehension Question. As with the Romans Invitation, it is important to ask your friend, "Have you clearly understood what I've said?"

If he or she has not, try to explain the areas that are not clear to your friend. Review the passages above until your friend is ready to proceed.

4. The Renewal Question. Ask, "Friend, how has your experience with the Lord been today? Do you feel the need to be renewed in Christ?" If your friend responds to the invitation for renewal, lead him or her in a simple renewal prayer based on WAR: Jesus, I *want* you to be in control of my life. I *ask* for your forgiveness and for you to take control. Please *renew* your control in my life right now.

After your friend prays, use verses Romans 8:1,2 for assurance. For example:

You: Friend, Romans 8:1,2 are very encouraging to us at this point of renewal. Would you read them out loud?

Friend: "Therefore, there is now no condemnation for those who are in Christ Jesus, because through Christ Jesus the law of the Spirit of life set me free from the law of sin and death."

You: According to verse 1, what is true about you?

Friend: I'm not under condemnation.

You: Whose law are you under now?

Friend: The law of the Spirit.

You: What has this law freed you from?

Friend: The law of sin and death.

You: Friend, I've enjoyed this time with you. Thank you for allowing me the opportunity to share these Scriptures with you.

Renewal Is Infectious

Helping Christian friends renew their lives in Jesus Christ

is an important aspect of FRIENDS evangelism. It is vital
that we teach believers to turn the control of their lives
over to the lordship of Jesus daily. We all fail. But realizing
the opportunity of continually renewing Christ's lordship in
our lives can make the difference between despair and
hope in the life of an individual. Personal renewal can also
make the difference between dreariness and excitement in
the life of a congregation.

Recently at a HELPER seminar, a pastor with a Ph.D.
and many years of experience in the ministry renewed his
life in Christ. When he returned to his congregation the
next week, he preached a sermon on the Romans Invitation, including the material on renewal included in this
chapter. He called the church officers and the entire congregation to consider renewing their lives in Christ. Many
made that decision. Several church officers realized that
they had never made a specific, conscious commitment to
Jesus Christ. They came to the pastor's office after the
service to pray together and confirm their commitment.
Others recognized a need to renew their commitment to
serve Jesus Christ.

A number of renewed church members decided to
meet on weekday mornings for prayer. They were all
working men and women, so the only practical time for
them to assemble was at 6:15 A.M. But their desire for
prayer was so intense that they asked that the church parlor be opened early five days a week for six weeks so they
could seek the Lord together. Family members of the
renewed Christians soon began attending worship to see
for themselves what was going on. An unprecedented
church renewal was under way!

As you learn to renew Christ's control in your life daily,
and teach your friends to do the same, think what could
happen in your church!

CHAPTER 7
The Three Circles of Christianity

*Jesus spoke all these things to the crowd
in parables; he did not say anything to
them without using a parable.*
Matthew 13:34

Jennifer, the boys and I were away from home taking two
weeks of vacation. We had a little kitchen where we were
staying, so every two or three days I drove to a nearby
grocery store to pick up bread, milk and hot dogs. After
gathering my supplies in the store, I purposely went
through the check-out line where a particular young man
bagged the groceries. This grocery store was different
from the stores in Cincinnati because the young man carried my bags to my car without even being asked! So each
time I shopped, I sought out this young man and we talked
together as he carried my groceries to the car.

After a few trips he got to know me—that I was a minister on vacation, that I had three boys and so on. One day
as we stood talking beside my car, I pointed to the store's
logo on the grocery bag—a smiley face. "I like that circle
with the smile on it," I said, "because I often use a smiley
face to tell people about God's love."

"Oh," he said, "is that right?"

"Yes, I use a smiley face to illustrate the familiar verse John 3:16, which says that God loved the world so much that He sent His only Son Jesus into the world. Then I use another circle to show how God feels about sin." The

Because each person we encounter is a unique individual in a unique situation, it is important for a Christian witness to be equipped with a variety of methods for a variety of situations.

trunk of the car was dusty from our vacation travels, so I drew a circle in the dust with my finger. Inside the circle I drew a simple frowning face. "You see, God loves people, but God hates sin."

Then I drew another circle with a cross inside it. "So the cross was the means by which Jesus Christ became the mediator between God and humanity, so that all who believe in Him might be saved."

The young man followed my presentation closely as I went on to describe the good news of the gospel using simple circles drawn in the dust. Seeing he was anxious to get back to work, I said that maybe we could talk again at another time. So we parted.

A couple of days later, Jennifer and I went to the store together to pick up snacks and soda pop. I was disappointed when my favorite grocery bagger was not at the check-out counter when we left. "He probably saw you coming and hid," Jennifer laughed. "Sometimes people don't want to be cornered by an evangelist, you know!"

We were in the parking lot heading toward the car when someone hollered from a distance, "Hey, Reverend

Ron!" My young friend hurried across the parking lot and met us at the car.

"I was hoping to see you again before you went back to Cincinnati," he began. "I just wanted to tell you that I've been talking to my mom's minister about some of the things you told me about. He showed me some verses in the Bible and we prayed together. I want to thank you for taking time to share the three circles with me, because now I'm a Christian, too!"

Variety and Flexibility

Because each person we encounter is a unique individual in a unique situation, it is important for a Christian witness to be equipped with a variety of methods for a variety of situations. It is also helpful to focus the attention of our friends by using visual aids such as a paper and pencil, a napkin, a paper place mat, a dusty automobile or whatever is at hand.

Even in a brief encounter with a stranger, it is possible to exercise the principles of FRIENDS evangelism. First, it is important to be friendly and find common ground by listening, noticing and expressing appreciation. Maybe a store clerk is flustered or distracted by the phone ringing or by other customers demanding immediate attention. You can be a friend by politely standing aside for someone in a rush or saying, "That's okay, answer the phone. I'm in no hurry." Express understanding and sympathy for the clerk's difficult situation: "You're really running in circles today; you could use another clerk to handle all this business."

Or perhaps you are making a last-minute run to the gas station or convenience store on a holiday weekend. You can let the people serving you know that you appreciate their service: "I really appreciate your being here at work on Christmas Eve, when you'd like to be home with your family."

> *Truth pictured is often truth communicated and remembered.*

Be ready to recognize and express appreciation for work well done: "I admire the efficient way you handle (whatever the work is). It's evident that you care about the work you do." By expressing honest appreciation and interest in the other person, you earn the right to be heard because you reveal the gospel first by your life. After interceding for the person, you may or may not find an opening to reveal the gospel with your lips. If an opening appears, nurture any response and seek to disciple the person through involvement with a local church fellowship.

Encircling Your Friends

Remember the story of the religious leaders who brought to Jesus a woman caught in adultery? They wanted to trap Jesus into condemning her, but Jesus trapped them in their hypocrisy instead. But while the leaders shouted their accusations, Jesus crouched down and drew figures on the ground. We don't know what Jesus drew or wrote on the ground, but it is interesting that He often used visual aids in His teaching—lilies, sparrows, fish, bread, stones, grain and figures drawn in the dust.

Truth pictured is often truth communicated and remembered. The Three Circles of Christianity approach is designed to reveal the truth of the gospel through simple illustrations and drawings. This method may be used conveniently to share the gospel with people you encounter briefly such as cab drivers, store clerks, flight attendants, waiters and waitresses and fellow passengers on a bus or plane. The entire presentation can be made in a few minutes or expanded into greater detail as time permits. The point is made quickly and effectively through the use of three circles and several familiar symbols.

Each point of the Three Circles approach is based directly on Scripture. The texts are listed here, but it is not necessary to have all the verses memorized for the presentation. Remember: This approach is especially suited for brief encounters when limited time does not allow for a detailed rendering of every text. Of course, if a Bible is available and if time permits, it is always helpful to turn to the appropriate passage and "read and review" it with the listener.

In the example below, Eileen has only a few minutes to share something of the good news with Fran.

1. The Introduction

Eileen: Fran, I would like to share with you something about Christianity that has been meaningful to me.

Fran: I'm interested, Eileen, but I don't have much time.

Eileen: This will only take a moment.

2. The Good News in Three Circles

Eileen: What I have to share can be summarized by these three circles. (Eileen draws three circles, one under the other. Then she draws a simple smiley face in the top circle.) This smiley face reminds us of the main message of the Bible, that God loves us. I'm sure you've heard

Figure 1   **Figure 2**

John 3:16 which says that God loves the entire world. That means God loves you, Fran (see Fig. 1).

Even though God loves us, the Bible tells us that *God hates sin*. (Eileen draws a frowning face in the second circle.) God's displeasure with sin is represented by an angry or sad face. The Bible tells us in Romans 3:23 and 6:23 that all of us have sinned and deserve God's punishment.

But in the first chapter of Romans, particularly in the *New International Version*, it is very clear that God's wrath is against ungodliness, not ungodly people. That's an important distinction. God hates sin, but He loves the sinner.

This third circle symbolizes the fact that God loved sinners—all of us—enough to send His own Son into the world to die on a cross for our sins. (Eileen draws a cross in the third circle which divides the circle into four sections.) Each of the four parts of the circle represents one important fact about Jesus Christ, the Son of God. Each fact begins with the letter *M*. (Eileen writes an *M* in each quarter of the circle.)

First, Jesus Christ became a *man*. This is the message of Christmas: God's Son came to earth and was born as a human baby to the virgin Mary.

Second, since Jesus was both God and man, He now serves as the perfect *mediator* between God and humanity. That means that Jesus came to bring sinners and the God who loves sinners together.

Third, Christ's cross became the *method* of bringing God and humanity together. The Bible says that the wages of sin is death. Jesus Christ received the wages our sin earned by His death on the Cross and thereby satisfied God's requirement for sin.

Fourth, Jesus Christ is now the *means* by which we are allowed to come to God. His birth, death and resurrection cleared the path for sinners to receive forgiveness from the God who loves them. Jesus said in John 14:6, "I am the way and the truth and the life. No one comes to the Father except through me."

3. Response to Christ in Three Circles

Eileen: The next three circles illustrate the three ways people respond to Christ. (Eileen draws three more circles aligned vertically.) The first circle represents the person who has received Jesus Christ by personal invitation and who relates to Jesus as the Lord of his or her life. (Eileen draws a small cross in the center of the top circle.) Christ has become the center of this person's life. He is both Savior and Lord. This person is a Christian, for the word Christian means "Christ-in-one"—Christ is in control of his or her life (see Fig. 2).

The second circle represents the person who has received Jesus Christ, but no longer allows Christ to occupy the center of his or her life. (Eileen draws a small, off-center cross in the second circle.) This person is a Christian, but he or she is not presently allowing Christ to be in control as Lord.

The third circle represents the person who has never received Jesus Christ into his or her life. (Eileen draws a small cross outside the bottom circle.) This person has never personally asked Christ to come and take control. Christ is outside of this life, seeking to enter.

4. The Clarifying Question

Eileen: There are three kinds of people in the world, Fran (see Fig. 3). Which one of these people would you say you are? (Eileen writes the letters *Y* and *U* beside each of the circles, forming the word "you" three times.) Where is Jesus Christ in relationship to your life? Is He in

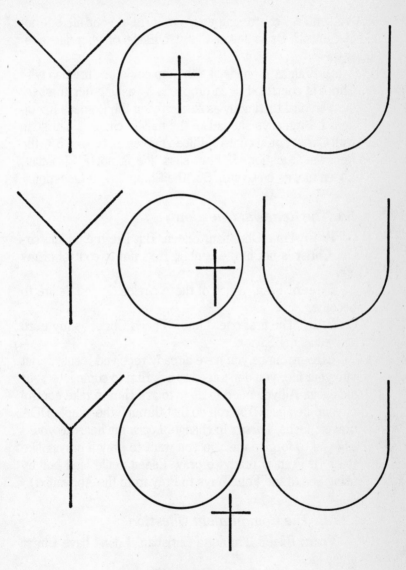

Figure 3

the center—controlling you? Or is He in your life but not in control? Or is Jesus Christ outside of your life altogether?

(If Fran says she is like the top circle, a Christian with Christ in control, Eileen proceeds by asking her to share her personal testimony as illustrated in the Romans Invitation. If Fran says she is like the middle circle, a Christian with Christ not in control, Eileen moves on to step 5A, the Renewal Question. If Fran says she is not a Christian, Eileen moves on to step 5B, the Commitment Question.)

5A. The Renewal Question

Fran: I'm a Christian, Eileen. But like the middle circle, Christ is not in the center; He's not in control of my life.

Eileen: Fran, which of these circles do you desire to become?

Fran: The first one. I know I need Christ as my Lord as well as my Savior.

Eileen: Since you have already received Jesus Christ into your life, you don't need to ask Him to come into your life again. All you need to do is to ask Him to take control of your life again. You can do that through the simple DOA prayer: Jesus, I *desire* to change. I *open* my heart to you. I *ask* you to forgive me. Do you want to pray a prayer like that? (If Fran is ready to pray, Eileen could lead her by using one of the Four Ways to Pray from the Appendix.)

5B. The Commitment Question

Fran: Eileen, I'm not a Christian. I don't have Christ in my life.

Eileen: Which of these circles do you desire to become?

Fran: The first one. I need to invite Christ into my life.

Eileen: That's wonderful, Fran. You can do so right now. All you need to do is to ask Him to come into your life and to take control of your life as He promised in the Bible. You can do that through this simple DOA prayer: Jesus, I *desire* to be a Christian. I *open* my heart to you. I *ask* you to forgive me. Do you want to pray a prayer like that? (If Fran is ready to pray without further encouragement, Eileen can help her by using one of the Four Ways to Pray from the Appendix.)

6. A Negative Response

If Fran does not want to accept Christ or pray, Eileen may tactfully ask, "Is there any good reason that would prevent you from asking Jesus Christ into your life?" Eileen should seek to determine if Fran has understood the gospel or if there are some underlying misunderstandings that prevent her from being open to Christ.

> *Those who are unwilling to make a commitment may be unripened fruit. Don't bruise green fruit! Your goal is to share the "how to," give an opportunity for the "to do" and then leave the "when to" to the Holy Spirit.*

When you receive a negative response, try to discover the reason, but do not pressure your friend. If there was a misunderstanding of the presentation, try to make it clear and give your friend another opportunity to receive Christ. If your friend still refuses, close by stating your hope that he or she will come to know Jesus Christ personally someday soon.

Those who are unwilling to make a commitment may be unripened fruit. Insensitivity to their needs may only make it more difficult for them to be open to the gospel at a later time. Don't bruise green fruit! Your goal is to share the "how to," give an opportunity for the "to do" and then leave the "when to" to the Holy Spirit.

Circles in the Soil

George, a member of our church, had been friends with Harold for many years. When Harold's wife died, George exercised his friendship by visiting, listening and offering comfort. Harold had looked forward to his retirement, spending time with his wife developing their garden, travelling and doing things they never had time to do. But their plans were cut short by her sickness and death. Harold wondered what was left for him in life. In his grief, Harold became open to talking about death, life after death and the meaning of living.

On one visit together the two men went out into Harold's lovely garden. Harold admitted with a tinge of bitterness that George's life seemed to become better since his retirement—his health seemed better, his wife seemed happier and he seemed to look forward to each new day.

George picked up a trowel and told Harold that he wanted to express a few thoughts about the joy Harold saw in his life. He bent down and began drawing circles in the soil with the trowel. He explained that God loves everyone and proved His love by sending His Son Jesus Christ. Jesus knew the sting of death, George comforted his friend, and He can identify with us in our grief and sorrow. George assured his friend that the Bible says that eternal life can belong to anyone who puts faith in Jesus and what He did for us on the cross.

George led Harold in a prayer of commitment to Jesus Christ that day. And he continued to lead his friend in studying the Scriptures, particularly the promises of comfort and eternal life.

Bacon and Eggs

Sam is a longtime member of our church who has completed our FRIENDS evangelism training. He had been trying to lead his friend Dwight into the Christian faith for several years. Finally an opportunity appeared one morning when they were having breakfast together before work. Dwight was complaining about some people who were bothering him at work. Sam decided to try something unusual to shift his friend's attention from his grievances to the underlying cause of his difficulties.

Sam ordered two fried eggs and three slices of bacon for breakfast. As he began talking to Dwight about the gospel, Sam made a smiley face on his plate by using the eggs for eyes and the bacon for a smiling mouth. Sam began to talk about the basic message of God's love, then he turned the bacon strips downward to illustrate God's sorrow over our sin—emphasizing Dwight's troubles at work were directly related to sin. Then Sam took two pieces of bacon and formed a cross over the plate, explaining what God did by sending Jesus Christ.

"Mmmm," Sam said as he ate the third strip of bacon. "I said 'mmmm' because there are four *M*s that stand for four facts about Jesus . . ." Sam continued with the Three Circles presentation, even using the position of the yellow eggs on the white plate to demonstrate the three types of individuals. Dwight gave Sam his full attention throughout. Sam's only difficulty was being unable to review his points because he ate the visual aids as he went along!

When the waiter brought the check, Dwight thought the presentation was over. But Sam said humorously, "Dwight, I want to pay for your breakfast today. I know you don't deserve it because you've been giving me a hard time. But I want to show you how Jesus pays the price for our sin even though we don't deserve it."

By the time they left the restaurant, Dwight was ready to put his faith in Jesus Christ. They sat together in Sam's car and prayed that the Holy Spirit would bring new life and light into every part of Dwight's life.

Variations on a Theme

Here are a couple of methods for sharing the good news which can be used in conjunction with the Three Circles or by themselves as the opportunity may dictate.

How About Some M & M's? In March 1984 I was invited to speak at an InterVarsity Christian Fellowship conference in Ft. Lauderdale. It was spring break for most colleges, which meant that tens of thousands of students from all over the United States converged on the Florida beaches. The InterVarsity students came to Ft. Lauderdale for a special purpose: to share Jesus Christ with as many vacationing students as possible. These would-be witnesses were eager to share their faith, but many of them lacked a witnessing plan. My assignment was to equip them with several effective methods for sharing their faith.

The method that really became popular was the M &

Ms approach. I encouraged these Christian students to buy some M & Ms candies and share them with strangers on the beach as an introduction. Once a conversation was started, the witnesses could use the candies to introduce their new friends to Jesus Christ—the *man*, the *mediator* and God's *method* and *means* for salvation.

The IV students swarmed into the local candy stores and bought out their supplies of M & Ms. Then they hit the beaches in teams of two and found it extremely easy and natural to offer M & Ms as a means of sharing the good news. The M & Ms presentation of the gospel always had "sweet" results!

Glasses of Living Water. Several lay people from our church were returning from a conference late one night, overflowing with joy from the beautiful worship and fellowship experiences. They stopped at a restaurant for a cup of coffee, commenting to the waitress that they appreciated finding a nice, clean place open so late. They placed their orders and went on with their joyous conversation, laughing and joking.

"My, you folks are happy tonight," the waitress said.

"Yes we are!" answered Linda. "Would you like to know why? Let me show you." Then she arranged three water glasses in a row on the table—one empty, one about half full and one filled to the brim.

"Look at these glasses," she began. "First, there are some people in this restaurant who are like this empty glass. They are created to hold the joy of the Lord, but they don't know Him. This second glass represents a person who is a Christian, but is not filled with the Spirit. When the Lord is within us, He fills us completely with joy, like this third glass that is filled with water. And if the full glass bumps against something, it spills over, just like we are spilling over with joy tonight."

The waitress shook her head. "But when you spill over, you're not full anymore. You're going to need to be filled up again."

Linda smiled. "That's exactly right. That's why Christians keep getting together to worship and pray. We need to continue to be filled with the Holy Spirit."

The waitress left to serve other customers, but a few minutes later she came back. "I'm on my break now. Would you tell me more about being filled with the Spirit?"

The group immediately agreed and made room for the waitress at the table. Linda and the waitress talked together for about 15 minutes, supported by the rest of the group at the table. The waitress, who said she hadn't been to church in seven years, expressed some of her doubts and disappointments about being a Christian. Linda talked about the three types of persons and the need to continually submit our lives to the lordship of Christ through renewal. When the waitress went back to work after her break, she too was filled to the brim with the joy and peace of the Holy Spirit.

As you can see from this chapter, the gospel can be revealed through simple, common illustrations such as circles in the dust, bacon and eggs, M & Ms and glasses of water. May we learn from the Master illustrator Himself who used common things to reveal the profound truth of God's love and plan of salvation for all.

CHAPTER 8
Come Unto Christ

Cast all your anxiety on him because he cares for you. 1 Peter 5:7
Come to me, all you who are weary and burdened, and I will give you rest.
Matthew 11:28

Lorraine Huston is a teller at a savings and loan bank in Cincinnati. One afternoon she was alone in the bank when a tall man in a long black coat walked in and approached her. He held his hand in his pocket as if he had a gun and ordered Lorraine to go into the back room and lie on the floor.

Lorraine was so frightened that she went into a rear restroom and locked herself in for 90 minutes. She finally crept out and called the police, but they were not at all sympathetic. Instead they were angry that she gave the criminal a 90 minute head start. When the story came out in the papers that night Lorraine felt even worse, fearing she might lose her job.

Lorraine's friend Thelma is a member of the College Hill Presbyterian Church and is trained in FRIENDS evangelism methods. When Thelma read the newspaper story, she drove immediately to Lorraine's house and found her alone and terribly upset. Thelma asked Lorraine to get her Bible while she put on some water for coffee. Then they

Sometimes people don't recognize their need of Jesus as their Saviour from sin. Sometimes their most pressing felt need is a personal problem, pain or crisis. They're looking for someone to meet them at the door of their concern and care.

sat together and read the verses of an evangelism approach called Come Unto Christ. As they talked, Lorraine admitted that she had always been afraid to open her heart to Jesus, thinking He might call her to preach, to become a missionary in the jungle or to give all her money away. She was sure that if she let Him have control of her life, something terrible would happen.

Thelma read aloud several passages about the love and gentleness of Jesus, but still Lorraine held back. Finally Thelma said, "Lorraine, I think you've locked the door of your heart just like you locked that restroom door at the bank. If you will just open the door of your heart, you will find someone who loves you—it's Jesus!"

After a few moments of thought, Lorraine prayed to receive Jesus into her heart and her fear and anxiety melted away.

The Door of Concerns and Cares

In Revelation 3:20 we discover that Jesus comes to us saying, "Here I am! I stand at the door and knock. If anyone hears my voice and opens the door, I will go in and eat with him, and he with me."

What door is Jesus referring to? Most evangelicals emphasize that Jesus knocks only on, and enters an individual's life through, the door of repentance from sin. But my experience in revealing Christ to others has persuaded me that this is not the only door Jesus approaches in individuals' lives. Sometimes people don't recognize their need of Jesus as their Savior from sin. Sometimes their most pressing felt need is a personal problem, pain or crisis. They're looking for someone to meet them at the door of their concern and care.

What does the voice of Jesus say at a person's heart's door? Sometimes He says, "Hello, sinner. Repent and I will come in." But some people are so buried in their problems that they don't see themselves as sinners in need of repentance. And so Jesus comes to the heart's door and says, "It's all right, fearful one. I've come to bring you peace," or "I am here with you, lonely one. I've come to bring you companionship."

In Matthew 11:28, Jesus said, "Come to me, all you who are weary and burdened, and I will give you rest." People suffer many burdens and needs which can become doorways for bringing them to Christ. Some come to Christ for comfort because of sorrow, for health because of sickness, for peace because of anxiety or for strength because of weakness. A person may come directly to Christ through any of these doors of need because He invites *all* who are weary and burdened to come unto Him.

We need to be very careful that we do not witness in an irresponsible way. Colossians 4:5,6 says that we are to be wise in the way we act toward those outside the faith. We are to be wise in our relationships with them so as not to give an unfavorable impression of the gospel. Instead we must cultivate wise conversation so we can speak appropriately to each individual and to the particular need of the moment.

Elizabeth, a deacon in our church, discovered this principle in her personal witnessing experience. She received her training in FRIENDS evangelism over 10 years ago and has frequently used these methods with her friends.

One of Elizabeth's witnessing projects over the years was her friend Marty. Earlier in their relationship, Elizabeth witnessed to Marty using an approach that centered on the issue of eternal life. The primary verses Elizabeth shared dealt with forgiveness of sin, inviting Christ into one's heart and assurance of God's acceptance. At that time Elizabeth invited Marty to come to Christ through the door of repentance.

But Marty responded by saying that she had dealt with those issues when she had a cancerous growth removed from her neck. Her answers indicated to Elizabeth that Marty did not have a personal relationship with Jesus Christ, but Marty was satisfied with her current level of commitment. Elizabeth respected Marty's decision and waited for another opportunity.

A few years later Elizabeth again drew close to Marty when her husband asked for a divorce. Marty was filled with anxiety about her self-worth, her finances and her family's future. The witnessing approach Elizabeth used years earlier was a good approach, but it was not the approach needed to meet Marty's new concern. It was not the door to forgiveness of sin or eternal life that Marty needed opened, but the door to abundant life in the face of her personal and marital crisis.

Because Elizabeth remained Marty's friend, she was there when Marty needed her. And because Elizabeth had learned a way to share Christ with her friends in their times of crisis, she was eventually able to lead Marty to a personal relationship with Jesus. When Elizabeth revealed her faith through the Come Unto Christ approach, Marty learned that her earlier answers to death and eternal life were inadequate and incorrect. The Holy Spirit revealed the truth to her and He continues to teach her today.

Inviting Concerned Friends to Come Unto Christ

As we seek to be friends when sharing the good news, we must be sensitive to the pressing needs our friends may be facing. As we hone in on those needs, we must rely on the Holy Spirit to guide us to meet those needs through Christ. The Come Unto Christ approach is designed to effectively minister to a friend with a specific need. Its emphasis is upon coming to Jesus Christ who is the answer to any need. Jesus is portrayed as the one who identifies with and personally cares for your friend.

It is good to be thoroughly familiar with the Direct Question/Logical Answer technique (described in chapter 4) and the content of the Scripture passages so that the logical sequence of the passages is clear. It is also helpful to set aside one particular copy of the New Testament, with key passages underlined, to be used solely for witnessing purposes. I write the page number of each successive passage to be used in the margin of my Bible so I can flip to it quickly. I also try to phrase each of the questions in my own words so the approach is personal and natural.

The following example illustrates how to use the Direct Question/Logical Answer technique with the Come Unto Christ approach of ministering to a hurting friend. The *New International Version* is used in this outline, but another translation may be substituted providing that it preserves the theme of each verse as found in the original Greek. The dialog is based on Elizabeth's ministry to Marty described earlier.

1. The Introduction

Elizabeth: Marty, I'm honored that you trust me enough to share your problem with me. I want to assure you that I care about you and will continue to be your friend no matter what happens in this situation. I also want you to know that God cares about your pain. I want to share some verses with you which tell us how we can depend on God in a situation like yours.

2. The Passages

Elizabeth: Look with me at 1 Peter 5:6. Will you read it out loud please?

Marty: "Humble yourselves, therefore, under God's mighty hand, that he may lift you up in due time."

Elizabeth: According to this verse, Marty, what will God do?

Marty: He will lift me up.

Elizabeth: When will God do it?

Marty: In His good time.

Elizabeth: Marty, please read that verse again. But this time insert your name when it refers to "yourselves" and "you" in the verse.

Marty: "Humble yourself Marty, therefore, under

God's mighty hand, that he may lift Marty up in due time."

Elizabeth: The next verse, 1 Peter 5:7, contains an amazing invitation. Read it for us.

Marty: "Cast all your anxiety on him because he cares for you."

Elizabeth: What does God invite us to do with our anxiety?

Marty: Cast it on Him.

Elizabeth: How much anxiety may we cast on Him?

Marty: All of it.

Elizabeth: Why should you give Him your anxiety?

Marty: Because He cares for me.

Elizabeth: Please read the verse out loud again, substituting your name for the personal pronouns.

Marty: "Cast all Marty's anxiety on him because he cares for Marty."

Elizabeth: The final verse I want to share with you contains a personal invitation. Please read Matthew 11:28.

Marty: "Come to me, all you who are weary and burdened, and I will give you rest."

Elizabeth: Marty, what is the invitation?

Marty: To come to Jesus.

Elizabeth: Who is invited?

Marty: All who are weary and burdened.

Elizabeth: What is the promise?

Marty: He will give them rest.

3. The Comprehension Question

Elizabeth: Have these verses been clear to you?

(If Marty answers no, Elizabeth reviews the verses and answers Marty's questions. If Marty understands the passages, Elizabeth moves on to the Clarifying Question.)

4. The Clarifying Question

Elizabeth: Marty, have you ever personally come to Christ and experienced Christ's caring for you?

(If Marty answers no, Elizabeth goes directly to the Commitment Question. If Marty answers yes, Elizabeth asks her to share her personal testimony. If Marty's commitment is indefinite, Elizabeth may use the President Example or the Marriage Example found in the Appendix. Then she moves on to the Concern Question.)

5A. The Concern Question

Elizabeth: Marty, would you like to come to Christ and commit this particular concern to Him?

Marty: Yes, I want to bring my concern to Christ.

(Elizabeth goes immediately to the Commitment Prayer. If Marty answers no to the Concern Question, Elizabeth asks if there is any particular reason Marty does not want to come to Christ with her problem.)

5B. The Commitment Question

Elizabeth: Would you like to come to Christ and personally experience His care for you?

Marty: Yes, I need Christ's care; I want to come to Him.

(Elizabeth goes to the Commitment Prayer. If Marty answers no, Elizabeth does her best to discover why Marty is unwilling to come to Christ.)

6. The Commitment Prayer

Elizabeth: Marty, you can state your commitment by praying a simple ABC. prayer: Lord, I *accept* your invitation. I *believe* in Jesus Christ and that He cares for me. I *come* now through faith in Him.

(If Marty does not want to pray, Elizabeth asks if there is a particular reason and deals with Marty's response.)

Friends Who Are Like Grandparents

Gary Stroup successfully avoided our deacons' visitation group for nine years, but he could not avoid a friend. Ila Mae, an older woman and longtime member of College Hill Presbyterian Church, was Gary's neighbor and sort of a grandmother to him.

He dropped into her kitchen one evening and shared some of his concerns and troubles. Being a good friend, and having been trained in FRIENDS evangelism, Ila Mae began to talk with him about Jesus Christ. Specifically, she asked why Gary had avoided church and what he really thought about God.

Gary answered by describing an event from early in his marriage when his infant daughter was killed in an automobile accident. Gary was angry with God. His anger turned into fear of what might happen to the rest of his family if he ever gave his life to the Lord.

Ila Mae has the sensitive wisdom one hopes to find in a grandmother. She also knows how to use the Scriptures because of her training in the Come Unto Christ approach. She ministered to Gary's need, acknowledging his hurt, grief and fear. When she reached the Commitment Question, Ila Mae said, "Gary, something tells me that you want to ask the Lord to take your hurt and pain, and to accept His invitation to come unto Him." With tears in his eyes, Gary knelt with Ila Mae to receive Christ.

Hunting for Jesus

Tom was a Vietnam veteran who had been dealt some bad cards in life. His mother died when he was young and his brother was sent to prison when he and Tom were in their

early 20s. Tom hinted that he had been involved at the
fringes of organized crime, but realized that there was no
future for him there. His war experience left him angry at
society and bitter about life.

I got involved with Tom in Minnesota through the common interest of hunting. Tom took every opportunity to
get out into the wilderness, feeling that shooting was
about the only way he could release the rage inside him.
Tom knew all the best goose pits and duck blinds, and for
some reason he took me to secret hunting spots that he
shared with no one else. We would go out into the woods
together and hunt for days.

In the course of our friendship Tom's father became
seriously ill at the same time Tom's wife was ready to
deliver twins. Tom was fearful that he would lose his
father, but he needed to be at his wife's bedside as well.
He always considered himself self-sufficient, but suddenly
he was powerless to help the two people he loved most
when both were in mortal danger.

Tom's heavy burden broke his self-reliance and he
wept as he poured out his heart to me. I had the opportunity to share with Tom the passages in the Come Unto
Christ approach. He discovered God's love and established a personal relationship with Christ by faith. I introduced Tom to some of the supportive Christian fellowships
at our church, shared with him what Christ meant to me in
times of crisis and taught him how he could let Christ bear
his anxieties.

Tom's wife gave birth to two healthy babies, a boy and
a girl. Although Tom's father lived only a few more
months, he did rejoice in the knowledge of his grandchil-
dren before he died. I saw a change in Tom in the months
that followed, because much of his anger and bitterness
was dissipated by the peace of Christ.

Hello, Can You Talk for a Minute?

The phone rang late one night after I was already asleep. It was Sharon White, a young woman who was on my first evangelism team years earlier in Mora, Minnesota. "Ron, I know it's late and I'm sorry to bother you," she began, obviously crying. "But I had to talk with somebody." I assured her that I cared, then settled in to listen to her troubles.

Sharon had just been jilted by her fiance. That would have been grief enough, but I knew she had experienced several other disappointing relationships and her self-esteem was falling very low. She said she felt like a boxer who had been knocked down so many times that it seemed stupid to struggle to her feet and try again.

After she poured out her pain and tears I said, "Sharon, go get your Bible."

She left the phone for a moment, came back and said, "I know just where you want me to turn; 1 Peter 5, right?"

"Right," I said, and we laughed. "I remember teaching these verses to you a long time ago, Sharon. And I remember that you used these verses to minister to people in Mora who were having personal problems. But why don't you go ahead and read verses 6 and 7 out loud."

"I know what you're going to say next," she laughed. "You want me to read those verses with my name in place of the pronouns."

"Right again," I said. Then I listened as she read the passage. Sharon's laughter turned to weeping as she was confronted by the Holy Spirit and His call for her to act on what she had often taught to others: to cast her cares on Christ, because He cared about her.

As illustrated with Sharon, the Come Unto Christ

approach can be used effectively over the telephone. When a friend calls with a concern, listen carefully. Then say, "I'd like to share with you a thought from the Bible about what you have said." Have your friend follow in his or her Bible as you read the verses and ask specific application questions about them.

Weighty Matters

In my office I have a visual aid that I often use with the Come Unto Christ approach. It's a 10-pound weight that I made by melting metal toothpaste tubes together (a class project from my school days).

One afternoon I was counseling a woman who was worrying herself sick about a particular problem. We went over the verse "Cast all your anxiety on Him" from 1 Peter 5:7, but she just couldn't seem to let go of her problem.

I asked her to stand up, and then I handed her the 10-pound weight. "Hold this with both hands straight out in front of you," I said. It wasn't easy for her because she was a petite woman with very thin arms. "Now we're going to pray. And when we say, 'I cast my cares on you, Jesus,' I want you to let go of that weight."

"You mean drop it?"

"Yes," I said. "When we pray, 'I cast my cares on you, Jesus,' you drop the weight."

So we prayed, and when we came to the line, "I cast my cares on you, Jesus," I paused, bracing myself for the thud. But nothing happened. I opened my eyes to see the woman still gripping the weight, her little arms trembling like they were going to break. Tears ran down her face. Her teeth were clenched and her knuckles were white with the strain of holding onto a problem she could not release. So I repeated very slowly, "Jesus, I cast this problem on you . . . *now!*"

She dropped that 10-pound metal weight and burst into tears. But when she walked out of my office that afternoon, she was refreshed and renewed because she had left her problem in Jesus' hands.

That woman reminds me of the crippled man at the pool of Bethesda in John 5:1-9. He had lain there for 38 years waiting to be healed! Jesus asked him, "Do you want

Sometimes we need to be very honest with the burdened friends we are inviting to Christ. Do they really want to let go of their problems? Or do their problems bring them attention, sympathy or a convenient excuse to be less than God wants them to be?

to get well?" But the man made excuses: no one would help him into the healing pool, so other cripples were healed instead of him.

Sometimes we need to be very honest with the burdened friends we are inviting to Christ. Do they really want to let go of their problems? Or do their problems bring them attention, sympathy or a convenient excuse to be less than God wants them to be? The crippled man sat at the pool of Bethesda for 38 years until Jesus asked him directly, "Do you want to get well?" Perhaps Jesus needs to ask our friends a similar question through us so that they might get moving!

Of course, none of us is immune to trials and crises in life. The Come Unto Christ passages not only minister to our friends in their personal needs, but they also minister to us in our moments of need. Are we tempted to cling to our problem using the same excuse as the cripple? "Well Lord, I would love to be a witness of your good news, a worker at the church, a better husband, a better neighbor. But, you see, I have this problem, so I can't."

Jesus comes to us at that point and asks, "Do you want to get well?" If we want to be effective in ministering Christ to our burdened friends, we must answer yes—and let go of the weight.

CHAPTER 9
Who Do You Say I Am?

"But what about you?" he asked. "Who do you say I am?" Peter answered, "You are the Christ." Mark 8:29

We have a custodian at College Hill Presbyterian Church whom everyone calls "Lovey." Lovey's nickname is appropriate because he is a very lovable guy. He's big enough to be a tackle on the Bengals' football team and he has a huge heart to match. And Lovey always wears a smile.

As a custodian, Lovey spends some of his time working in the kitchen during our HELPER seminars. One evening Lovey was in the kitchen with his friend Chuck Bergerman, one of our church members. In the adjoining room our seminar group was singing "Praise the Name of Jesus" and Lovey was humming along. "I've known you for a long time, Lovey," Chuck said, "and we've done a lot of things together. But there's one thing about you I don't know. Do you have a personal relationship with Jesus?"

Lovey said he knew that Jesus was the Son of God and that He died on the cross for our sins. They talked some more, then Chuck picked up a Bible (we have Bibles and New Testaments stashed in all our church rooms). Chuck said, "One of the things Jesus asked His disciples was 'Who do you say I am?' He had been with them a long time and He wanted to make sure they really knew Him."

Chuck used several passages to point out that Jesus wanted each individual to know Him personally as Lord and Savior. The conversation ended with Lovey stating that he wanted to ask Jesus to be his personal Savior and Lord. Chuck led Lovey through a prayer of commitment.

Chuck's ministry to Lovey is a perfect example of FRIENDS evangelism. Chuck found common ground with Lovey and became his friend, earning the right to be heard. Chuck revealed the gospel through his life. He knew that many at the church had been interceding for Lovey, so he took the opportunity to express the gospel through his lips using a method we call Who Do You Say I Am?

We see people sitting in church, singing in the choir, coming to Sunday School and special services. We assume that they are Christians too, but it's not always so. Often we assume too much.

Chuck also joyfully accepted the responsibility of nurturing and discipling Lovey, helping him understand his faith and taking time to study the Bible with him. Some members of Lovey's family have become interested in learning more about Jesus Christ through Chuck's ministry. That's what FRIENDS evangelism is all about.

Do We Assume Too Much?

Many people at College Hill probably assumed that Lovey was a Christian all along. After all, he was employed by the church. Similarly, we see people sitting in church, singing in the choir, coming to Sunday School and special services. We assume that they are Christians too, but it's not always so. Often we assume too much.

In chapter 1 I described how I committed my life to Christ as a young teenager through the ministry of Rev. Neal Kamp. On the evening of my commitment I told my parents what I had done. Then I asked them why they had not introduced me to Christ themselves. I will never forget that moment. Tears welled up in their eyes and my dad said, "Ron, we assumed too much; we thought you were already a Christian." Then we prayed together and thanked the Lord for all that He had done for me through them and others.

At a HELPER seminar in Bloomington, Indiana, I gave my personal testimony and told about my father's sorrow at assuming too much about my faith. After the Saturday morning session, an elder in that church went home to eat with his family instead of eating the supper provided at the seminar. He took the opportunity to talk to his 12-year-old son about Jesus Christ using one of the methods he learned at the seminar. He also shared his personal testimony. His son was moved, admitting that he saw Christ in his dad's life and that he was glad his dad shared with him. The boy asked if he could pray to receive Jesus Christ as his own personal Savior and his father led him in a prayer of commitment right then and there.

When the elder returned to the church for the evening session, he stood up and told us his exciting story. He had tears in his eyes as he said, "I was an assuming parent also. But thanks to your openness with your testimony, Ron, I had the joy of leading my own son to the Lord today."

Making Known the Unknown

In Arlington National Cemetery outside Washington, D.C. stands the Tomb of the Unknown Soldier. This monument, containing the remains of an unidentified military man, is representatively dedicated to many nameless soldiers who gave their lives so that our nation might live in freedom. We don't know the name of the unknown soldier, but at least we have an idea of what he—and thousands like him—have done for us.

Jesus Christ is often described in the Bible in military terms. He is called the Lord of Hosts, our Victor in the war against sin and death. He shed His blood and gave His life so that people of every race and nation might be free from sin and live in peace with God.

But to millions of people across the world Jesus is an unknown soldier. He fought the ultimate battle and won their freedom from sin. But they don't know His name; they don't even know what He did for them.

Even when Jesus walked on earth He was unknown to most people: "He was in the world, and though the world was made through him, the world did not recognize him. He came to that which was his own, but his own did not receive him" (John 1:10,11). Even His own people, the Jews who were waiting for the promised Messiah, did not recognize Jesus as the Christ.

On one occasion, described in Mark 8:27-29, Jesus asked His closest followers, "Who do people say I am?" The disciples gave a variety of answers—all wrong. It was only when Jesus personalized the question—"Who do *you* say I am?" (italics added)—that the correct answer was given. Peter, who was often the spokesperson for the disciples, responded by identifying Jesus as Christ the Messiah, the promised Redeemer of God.

> *The Bible was written to give us the correct answer to the question Jesus asks all of us: "Who do you say I am?"*

At Lazarus' tomb Jesus asked Martha a similar question leading to the proclamation of His true identity. Martha correctly responded, "I believe that you are the Christ, the Son of God, who was to come into the world" (John 11:27). The Holy Spirit gave Peter and Martha ears to hear and eyes to recognize that Jesus was the Divine Deliverer.

The Bible was written to give us the correct answer to the question Jesus asks all of us: "Who do you say I am?" The Old Testament identifies Him as the promised Messiah who was *coming* to the world. The New Testament identifies Him as the Messiah who *has come* and fulfilled every promise made by God.

The Who Do You Say I Am? witnessing approach focuses on the discovery of who Jesus is, what He has done and how one can know Him personally. It can be used to share the gospel with anyone, even those who have never heard of Jesus. But it is especially effective when confronting people like Lovey whom we may assume have already committed their lives to Christ. Who Do You Say I Am? brings individuals face to face with the Lamb of God who takes away the sin of the world.

1. The Bible Purpose Question

You: Friend, may I ask you a question about the Bible? In your understanding, why was the Bible was written?

(Your friend's answer may or may not give you insight into his or her personal faith. But affirm whatever answer is given, even if only to say, "That's very interesting; I never thought of it that way before." Then continue.)

You: Let's look at how the Bible states its purpose. Look with me at John 20:30,31. Please take the Bible and read the passage out loud.

Friend: "Jesus did many other miraculous signs in the presence of his disciples, which are not recorded in this book. But these are written that you may believe that Jesus is the Christ, the Son of God, and that by believing you may have life in his name."

You: Even though the Bible's stated purpose is that people believe in Christ, many people do not know who Jesus Christ is nor why He came. Even when He was on earth people disagreed about who He was. Once He asked His disciples who people thought He was and they gave several different answers—a great prophet, a great teacher or a leader.

2. The Identification Question

You: Friend, if someone asked you, "Who do you say Jesus is?" what would you answer?

(If your friend's answer reveals personal faith in Jesus as Savior, ask your friend to share with you how he or she came to know Christ as personal Savior. But if your friend's responses suggest that he or she has not made a personal commitment to Jesus Christ, proceed with the dialogue below.)

You: Let's look at how your answer compares with the statements about Jesus Christ in the Gospels. Would you turn with me to John 1:6-8 and read the verses aloud?

Friend: "There came a man who was sent from God; his name was John. He came as a witness to testify concerning that light, so that through him all men might believe. He himself was not the light; he came only as a witness to the light."

You: Here we see that John the Baptist was sent by God to be a witness to Jesus Christ. John's basic testimony is found in verse 29. Please read it for us.

Friend: "Look, the Lamb of God, who takes away the sin of the world!"

You: John the Baptist used the Jewish image of the Lamb of God to identify Jesus. You may know the story of how God freed the Jewish nation from slavery to Egypt. On the night they were to leave Egypt, the Jews were instructed by God to kill an unblemished lamb and put its blood on their doorposts so that the angel of death would pass over their homes. This led to their release from bondage and their establishment as a nation. The Passover is celebrated by Jews to this day.

In the Passover rites, the lamb of God is associated with atonement for sin. At the time of Jesus, the Israelites who celebrated the Passover sacrificed lambs without blemish and used the blood as an atonement for their sins. This act had to be repeated every year. The Old Testament states that the blood of the lamb covered the people's sins for that year. Hebrews 9:22 states, "Without the shedding of blood there is no forgiveness."

In the Scripture passage we just read, John the Baptist said that Jesus Christ was the Lamb of God, the one God sent into the world as His sacrificial Lamb. He is without blemish, and He shed His blood and died for the forgiveness of the world's sin once and for all.

In the Old Testament, the lamb's blood only *covered*

the sins of the people. But in verse 29 John said that Jesus'
blood *takes away* sin once and for all. This means that God
has sent Jesus into the world to die for all the sins of
everyone, including my sins and your sins.

Let's look at two more verses. Follow along as I read
John 1:11,12: "He came to that which was his own, but his
own did not receive him. Yet to all who received him, to
those who believed in his name, he gave the right to
become children of God."

We see here that Jesus came to His own people, but
He was not accepted by everyone. There were those who
would not believe that He was the Lamb of God. However, verse 12 tells us that there were those who did
believe that He was the Lamb of God and received Him as
the one who could take away their sins. God gave to all
those who received Christ the right to become His children. All they need to do is to believe in Him and receive
Him.

3. The Comprehension Question

You: Friend, do you understand this summary of who
Jesus is and why He came?

(If your friend has any questions, you may answer
them by reviewing the verses. If he or she indicates an
understanding of the presentation, move to the Clarifying
Question.)

4. The Clarifying Question

You: Friend, a moment ago I gave you a Bible and you
opened your hand and received it. That act illustrates what
we must do with Jesus. We discovered that the Bible was
written to reveal who Jesus Christ is and why He came.
We also discovered that we need to receive Him personally as the one who has come to take away our sins. Have

you ever accepted Jesus Christ as your own personal Savior, the one who has come to take away your sins?

(If your friend answers yes, ask for a personal testimony and introduce the Renewal Approach if necessary. If he or she answers no, move directly to the Commitment Question.)

5. The Commitment Question

You: Friend, would you like to do that right now? Let me lead you in a simple prayer based on the letters CAR: Jesus, I want to become a *child of God*. I *acknowledge* that you are the Lamb of God who takes away the sins of the world. I *receive* you as my own personal Savior.

6. Immediate Follow-up

You: Friend, let's look again at verse 12. In your prayer you welcomed and received Jesus Christ. What did you become the moment you received Him?

Friend: A child of God.

You: That's right. You are now a member of God's family. Let's also look at verse 29. When you prayed and received Jesus as your personal Lamb of God, what did He do with your sin?

Friend: He took it away.

Living a Lie

I got to know Jim and Sandy through the baseball ministry at College Hill. Their son Jason was one of my best pitchers and Jim worked with me for three years as a coach.

Jim and Sandy invited me to a restaurant for lunch one day to share some of their personal problems. I was surprised when Jim revealed that Jason was his son from a former marriage and that he and Sandy were living together but not married. They were uncomfortable about their illicit arrangement because their friends among the other parents on the ball team, including us, assumed they were married. Jim and Sandy felt that their friendship with these parents was not completely honest.

I used my chef's salad as a visual aid to suggest that in some ways their lives were like the lettuce in the bowl—shredded by their circumstances. There was a variety of ingredients mixed together in their background which caused hurt and distrust, and stirred up confused feelings. They couldn't seem to sort everything out, so they tried to push all their problems under the surface. But something always happened to toss them all out again.

By comparing their problems to my salad, I was able to get them laughing and help them look at their situation from a new perspective. Then I wondered if I had been assuming something else about them. I didn't know for sure if they had committed their lives to Christ. So I used the Who Do You Say I Am? approach to ask them who they thought Jesus was and why they thought He had come to this earth.

Sandy said that she had come into a new awareness of Jesus' love, grace and acceptance from listening to the five-minute Bible studies I had with the ball players. She said it was this understanding of God's grace that led them to talk openly with me. We talked for quite awhile, but Jim and Sandy didn't feel ready to pray in the restaurant. I paid the bill and we walked outside by a rose garden with a bubbling fountain.

I told Sandy and Jim that the fountain reminded me of when Jesus was talking to the Samaritan woman at the well as described in John 4. That woman also had marriage problems that had drained of happiness and joy. But Jesus said that He would give her rivers of living water.

As we concluded our discussion beside the fountain, Sandy and Jim decided to accept Jesus as their Savior just as the woman at the well had received Him. They prayed and received Christ as their Savior from all past sins, and He washed their shame and their guilt away as well.

Shortly thereafter I performed the wedding for Jim and Sandy in the parlor of our church. Their son Jason was the best man.

Friends Indeed to Those in Need

Warren Akkerman was the manager of a large corporation in Cincinnati when he was suddenly stricken with multiple sclerosis. During his declining health, Warren lived with his two sisters Judy and Ruth who chose to care for their bedfast brother in their home instead of hospitalizing him.

Bill and Augusta Gibson are members of our church and were neighbors of the Akkermans. Bill is mechanically minded and often helped the Akkermans by repairing light switches, unclogging clogged drains and performing other home repairs. Augusta enjoyed baking and sewing, so she used her skills to provide special taste treats and little cross-stitched gifts to cheer and encourage her neighbors during their difficult days.

As their friendship grew over the years, the Akkermans asked the Gibsons about their church involvement. The Gibsons invited Judy and Ruth to come to church with them. They came and enjoyed the service, but were overwhelmed by the size of the congregation and the number of activities printed in the bulletin. They felt it would be

difficult to become involved, especially since so much of
their time was spent caring for Warren.

Bill and Augusta continued to share their love and
friendship. As questions about religion came up, they tried
to answer by referring to the Bible, particularly passages
explaining who Jesus Christ is. They introduced the
Akkermans to the Jesus who heals, who comforts in suffering and who brings patience and joy in the midst of great
tribulation to the bedridden and those who give themselves to care for them.

It was the Gibsons' witness of who Jesus is, presented
in the warmth of their loving friendship, that captured the
hearts of the Akkermans. "We now know why you are able
to serve the way you do," Judy told Augusta. "We saw the
love in your church, just as we see it in you. You have
shown love to us continually, without getting tired or for-
getting about us. How can we ignore that? We need that
kind of love in our own lives." Together Warren, Judy and
Ruth prayed to ask Jesus Christ to be their Savior and fill
their lives with the joy they saw in the Gibsons.

> *There are people all around us who have
> not found the correct answer to Jesus'
> question, "Who do you say I am?" We must
> extend our friendship and express our faith
> so they too may know the Lamb of God
> who takes away their sin.*

Judy and Ruth began attending worship services regularly, but they avoided other activities because they felt
that their ministry was to care for their brother. Warren
became a member of the church through correspondence,
eagerly listening to tapes of the new members' class, ser-

mons and other Christian education lessons. He became a witness himself by making tapes of his testimony to share with others. He committed himself to pray daily for our church staff. We were greatly encouraged as staff members to know that at least one person was praying specifically for us every morning.

When Warren went home to be with Jesus, Judy and Ruth moved west to live near other members of their family. But their lives were touched and transformed through the friendship and witness of loving neighbors. And we know that Judy and Ruth Akkerman continue their ministry to others through the joy of Jesus Christ in their lives.

There are people all around us who have not found the correct answer to Jesus' question, "Who do you say I am?" We dare not assume that our friends, neighbors, family members and fellow church attenders are personally committed to Christ. Rather we must extend our friendship and express our faith so they too may know the Lamb of God who takes away their sin.

CHAPTER 10
Pamphlets and Personal Testimonies

The scroll of the prophet Isaiah was handed to him. Unrolling it, he found the place where it is written: The Spirit of the LORD is on me, because he has anointed me to preach good news to the poor.
Luke 4:17,18

Leah Livingston, a member of our church, did not like using tracts or pamphlets to witness to people. She communicated her dislike to me more than once during her FRIENDS evangelism training in preparation for membership. "Tracts are like TV dinners: warmed-over spiritual food!" she objected. "When I share the good news with a friend, I want that person to know that it's coming right from my heart."

Leah is one of our lay teachers. She is experienced and skilled in witnessing and in teaching others to witness. In fact, Leah has taught members of our FRIENDS evangelism classes how to effectively use pamphlets. But she always made it clear that she did not like to use pamphlets herself.

One evening Leah was in the church kitchen helping

the caterer clean up after an evangelism training seminar.
The caterer's assistant, an older woman named Alice,
asked what the seminar was all about.

"We're teaching people how to share their personal
relationship with the Lord," Leah replied.

"I don't have a personal relationship with God, that's
for sure!" Alice confessed as she finished up her work.
"He's way up there and I'm way down here, and the twain
shall never meet."

Alice slipped on her coat to leave and Leah knew she
needed to share something quickly. A pamphlet explaining
the ABCs of Christianity had been left on the kitchen
counter after the seminar. Leah picked up the pamphlet—
the very one she told me she disliked—and began using it
to share the gospel with Alice, who listened with interest.

"But what about all the ornery things we do?" Alice
protested. "How can God ignore all that trash?"

Leah explained that God does not ignore our sin, He
forgives our sin because of what Jesus has done on the
cross. She turned another page and read how Jesus' death
is the means for our salvation and forgiveness.

*Pamphlets are excellent tools for witness-
ing, especially for Christians who are just
beginning to share their faith.*

Alice began to weep as she admitted her need of God's
forgiveness. Leah put her arm around Alice as she continued to share, and the old woman wept even more. Leah's
hand trembled as she turned to the last page and asked
Alice if she would like to ask Jesus to forgive her and fill
her with His comfort and peace. Alice eagerly said yes and
the two women prayed together.

Leah now has a different approach to teaching the pamphlet session in our training seminar. She learned firsthand that the Lord can even use a pamphlet as an effective tool to communicate His love.

Presenting Christ in a Pamphlet

Pamphlets are excellent tools for witnessing, especially for Christians who are just beginning to share their faith. Most pamphlets are self-contained summaries of the basic gospel message. Scripture passages are often printed in the pamphlets so you don't need a Bible at hand. Often the necessary transitions from one point to another, including comprehension questions, clarifying questions and commitment questions, are prepared for you in the pamphlet. Presenting Christ through a pamphlet is one of the easiest witnessing methods to learn and to use. Several specific pamphlets are recommended in the Appendix.

I use the word PAMPHLETS as an acrostic to list several helpful principles for witnessing with pamphlets and tracts:

> **P—Pray** for an opportunity to witness to your friends.
>
> **A—Ask** a leading question such as, "Have you seen this little booklet?" Or *announce* that the pamphlet has been meaningful to you and that you would like to share it with your friend.
>
> **M—Memorize** the pamphlet or at least its main points.
>
> **P—Personalize** it by using your friend's name as you share it and by looking at your friend and speaking from memory.

H—Hold the pamphlet in your hand where your friend can read it with you. Otherwise your friend may leaf through the pages too fast and lose the focus of the message.

L—Let your index finger "do the walking" and point out interesting illustrations or important words or phrases.

E—Extend an invitation to make a commitment to Christ after you have finished the pamphlet.

T—Thank your friend for allowing you to communicate your faith in this manner.

S—Seek to follow up your conversation with other conversations about the meaning of personal commitment to Christ.

What Do the Pros Use? Lilly Brown is a gifted and appreciated teacher in our adult Christian Education program. She has studied under some of the best theologians in the country and has taught the concepts of the Old and New Testament to hundreds of lay people over the years. But up until recently Lilly had never personally led anyone to Jesus Christ.

Lilly's longtime neighbor and friend had been attending church with her for some time. On the way out of church one Sunday the neighbor said, "The sermon was about a personal relationship with Christ. I don't think I have anything like that. How can I get to know God like that?"

Lilly the great Bible teacher was at a loss for words. She invited her friend into one of the staff offices and rummaged through her purse until she found a copy of the pamphlet *The Four Spiritual Laws*. Together they read each page and Lilly creatively explained and illustrated each point. Instead of reading the verses printed in the pamphlet, Lilly asked her neighbor to read them directly from the Bible. In this way she communicated that the pamphlet was a summary of what God said in the Scriptures.

In response to Lilly's friendship over the years and her clear, gentle presentation that morning, her neighbor prayed to accept Jesus Christ as her Lord and Savior. Lilly came out of the office floating on air. She was so happy! Later she told me, "I have enjoyed teaching many people about Christ, but the joy of leading someone to Jesus is the greatest!"

Lilly's experience with her neighbor opened the door to other witnessing experiences. She began utilizing her theological training to help her students understand how they can have a personal relationship with Jesus Christ.

Four Spiritual Laws Gold. Remember the color of the first edition of *The Four Spiritual Laws* pamphlet from Campus Crusade for Christ? It was kind of a highway stripe gold. Some years ago I purchased a '71 Ford Torino which was painted the same color. The Four Spiritual Laws was one of the first methods of witnessing I learned. And that gold Torino was one of my favorite "hooks" for introducing a gospel presentation.

One summer I was invited to speak at Grindstone Bible Camp in Minnesota. I arrived early to visit with the students and one young man, eyeing my Torino curiously, asked, "What kind of a color is that?"

"That's Four Spiritual Laws gold" I answered proudly.

"What?" he exclaimed in disbelief.

"Four Spiritual Laws gold," I repeated. "Haven't you ever heard of the Four Spiritual Laws?" I took the pamphlet from my pocket and laid it on the hood of my car. The colors matched perfectly. I led him through the four laws and he prayed to receive Jesus Christ on the spot. I corresponded with him through the summer and helped him start growing as a disciple of Jesus Christ.

Bridge Over Troubled Waters. Another pamphlet I use often is titled, *The Bridge to Life*, published by the Navigators. I often introduce the pamphlet with a story about the I-75 bridge in Cincinnati which spans the Ohio River, the border between Ohio and Kentucky.

Our son Nathan loves airplanes and is thinking about attending the Air Force Academy and pursuing a career in the Air Force or the space program. At the encouragement of a school friend, Nathan joined the Civil Air Patrol squadron in Covington, Kentucky, which is about 25 minutes from our home across the I-75 bridge. But after getting involved in the Covington squadron, Nathan discovered some benefits to belonging to the Cincinnati squadron. So he applied for a transfer.

Thanks to the I-75 bridge, Cincinnati and Covington are so close that we often consider them one metropolitan area. You may think that transferring from one squadron to another only a half hour apart is no problem. But the two squadrons have two separate commanders in two separate cities and in two separate states. In spite of the I-75 bridge, Nathan's transfer was a complicated procedure which took weeks to complete.

As the Navigators' pamphlet explains, Jesus Christ is the bridge God has constructed which transfers us from the kingdom of darkness into the kingdom of light (see Col. 1:13). We cannot transfer ourselves.

Unexpected Results. During a FRIENDS evangelism training session for new members, I asked for a volunteer to come forward and play the role of the listener while I demonstrated how to share Christ through a pamphlet. Keith Steinhauser came forward. Keith's parents had been members of our church for years and Keith attended Sunday School at College Hill as a child. After several years away in college and the Navy, Keith returned to Cincinnati and decided to become a member of College Hill Presbyterian Church. Even though he had a long history with our church, he was attending the new members' class for the first time.

I directed Keith through the pamphlet speaking as one friend to another. As I do in "real" witnessing situations, I asked Keith's permission to share a meaningful message from the Bible as summarized in a pamphlet.

We looked at the first pages and I pointed to the words with my index finger. I asked Keith to read the Scripture verses out loud using his own name instead of the pronouns. As Keith read the verses his voice began to quaver and tears filled his eyes. I suddenly realized we were no longer role playing. Keith was actually personalizing the Scriptures to his life.

It was as if Keith and I were alone in a desert and he had just discovered water for his thirsty soul. I moved my stool a little closer to him and put my arm around him as he read. When it came time to ask the question, "Was the information in this pamphlet meaningful to you?" I already knew Keith's answer. God was speaking to Keith through the pamphlet about something specific in his life.

Keith looked at me and the tears streamed down his face. He wept for some time, then I asked, "Keith, would you like to come to Christ and give Him the concerns He has been speaking to you about?"

"Yes I would," he responded.

I led Keith in a prayer of commitment. Then I invited the entire class to join in praying, singing and praising

God. As we left our subject matter and turned our hearts toward Jesus, other class members also committed their cares into the Lord's hands. God used a simple pamphlet and a hungry heart to spark a mini-revival in our class.

In Any Tongue. I designed a special pamphlet titled *Help* which has been translated into several different languages. *Help* communicates a simple gospel message through repetition and delightful illustrations prepared by an artist in our church.

I was asked by the Overseas Missionary Society to conduct an evangelism seminar for pastors and lay people in Haiti. Five of our lay people accompanied me on this seminar and we took along copies of the French version of *Help*, called *Au Secours*. We learned a couple of phrases in French so we could go out witnessing with the seminar participants. It was a wonderful experience because we did not speak the language and yet we saw the Holy Spirit work through us.

Our team demonstrated how to share with others by going to the busy marketplace. We would select an individual and ask in halting French, "Would you please help me by reading this booklet out loud?" As soon as the person began reading, a small crowd would surround us. The person reading the booklet was actually witnessing to his or her own people. We pointed to the illustrations and asked, "Which person would you like to be?" When people prayed to accept Christ, we immediately introduced them to the local pastor who was with us.

In January 1980 I was invited to bring a group of lay persons to Mexico City to conduct a HELPER seminar for pastors, seminary students and lay people. We used the same training methods we used in Haiti, but distributed a Spanish version of the pamphlet, *Soccorro*. Twenty-six of the 150 people who attended were members of the host church. In the year after our seminar, the membership of the host church doubled, then tripled and then quadrupled! The pastor told us that many families joined the church because the pictures in the pamphlet appealed to children and the message was so easily understood. We witnessed similar results in Brazil with the Portuguese version, *Ajuda.*

Our church periodically sends teams of witnesses to Haiti and Mexico, and these teams are equipped to share the good news through the *Help* pamphlet. When we witness this way, we always bring a pastor or lay person from a local church with us. In this way we train local Christians in evangelism and link new believers immediately with a supportive church. We are continually inspired by how God uses us in spite of language and cultural differences. His gospel overcomes all obstacles.

Presenting Christ in a Personal Testimony

As illustrated in the previous paragraphs, the good news in printed form is a marvelous evangelistic tool. But sometimes a personal message in the form of a testimony and verbal witness has a distinct advantage over the printed medium.

No Tracts, Just Facts. One hot Saturday afternoon a tall man with greasy black hair, scars on his face and a tattoo on his arm pushed his way past my frightened secretary and swaggered into my office. I invited him to sit down, trying to appear calm even though my heart was racing with fear.

He said his name was Joe. He had questions and he

wanted answers. "Who is God? What is Christianity all about? What does it mean to be saved?" I started to share with Joe from one of my handy tracts but he abruptly cut me off.

"You're the pastor of this church aren't you? You've been to seminary and earned your degree?"

> *Every Christian has a story to tell. You can share your own unique, individual experience with Jesus Christ. Your personal testimony is a meaningful way by which you can reveal "the good news according to you."*

"Yes, Joe," I said. "In fact, Presbyterian requirements for ordination are rather strict. I had to learn Greek and Hebrew and many other things. I have a doctorate in ministry."

"Well then," he snorted, "you should know enough to tell me about God without leaning on that little 10-cent tract! Why don't you just put down the props and tell me what you know about God?" I rose to Joe's interesting challenge and we talked about God for two hours.

At the end of our conversation Joe whipped a six-inch knife out of his pocket, deftly spun it around in his fingers and flipped it onto my desk. With my eyes bulging, Joe told me his story. He had come to my office from a street fight in a rough section of town. During the scuffle he was about to pull his knife and stab his opponent when a police officer broke up the ruckus. "I was so angry I really wanted to kill somebody," Joe hissed. "But if I had pulled the knife, the cop might have shot me. That scared me, so I decided to hand this knife over to someone I could trust to protect myself from what I might do."

Joe did not become a Christian until several years later. Now when we meet, we laugh about how he scared my secretary and terrified me when he flipped his knife onto my desk. But most of all we rejoice in our relationships with each other and with Jesus Christ.

The ABCs of a Personal Testimony

Every Christian has a story to tell. You may not have turned to Christ from a life of sordid crime like my friend Joe. But you can share your own unique, individual experience with Jesus Christ. Your personal testimony is a meaningful way by which you can reveal "the good news according to you."

Personal testimonies are useful for accomplishing one of two purposes with our friends: their personal encouragement and their personal commitment to Christ. The following principles are the ABCs of developing your personal testimony as a means of witnessing for encouragement or commitment:

> **A—Ask** the Holy Spirit to guide the selection and preparation of the words you speak (see Luke 12:12). **B—Be brief** and to the point. Be brief about your past way of life. Identify the roots instead of the fruits of past problems. For example, a divorce is the root of the problem while all the events surrounding the divorce are the fruits. A blow-by-blow description of all the events is inappropriate.
>
> Be brief and real about your present walk with Christ. Identify the struggles in your Christian walk as well as the successes. A

proper formula is $S = S$: share an equal number of successes and struggles in your testimony. Also be sure to keep your testimony fresh and updated. Include what God is doing now in your walk with Him and how He is changing your life.

Be brief and optimistic about your future with Christ. Identify a passage of Scripture that gives you a positive outlook in your future with the Lord. **C—Center** on Christ, not yourself. You must talk about yourself because it is your experience that you are describing. But be careful not to neglect Jesus, the one who has changed your life. A good formula is one "I" statement for each "Christ" statement.

Three to five minutes is a good target length for a personal testimony. This means that we need to spend a lot of time in prayer and preparation for each minute we speak, perhaps one hour of prayer for each minute of testimony.

The following step-by-step format will serve as a helpful guide for preparing and presenting your testimony:

1. An introduction. For example, you may say, "I would like to share something with you that has been very meaningful to me."

2. A comment about your past. Share something of what Christ did for you and how it happened.

3. A comment about your present. Include your struggles and successes and how Christ is meeting your needs.

4. A comment about your future. This may include a closing Scripture passage. If the testimony is intended to lead a friend to Christ, continue with the questions below.

5. The Comprehension Question. For example, "Has everything I've said been clear to you?"

6. The Clarifying Question. For example, "Have you

ever come to know Christ personally?"

7. *The Commitment Question.* For example, "Do you want to come to know Christ personally now?"

To Be or Not to Be. Jim and Carol Bolin attended our new members class in 1979. At the end of the series Jim told me he enjoyed the classes very much and felt they had been well worthwhile. But while Carol put her faith in Jesus Christ and became a member of our church, Jim said he wasn't ready to take that "bold leap of faith." I accepted his decision and told him I still wanted to be his friend.

Jim is an executive with a national corporation and his work takes him on the road often. When he was out of town Jim would drop me a letter so we could keep in touch. When he was in town he visited the new members class and I often asked him to give his "testimony." I wanted him to state clearly to the class that people can "agree to disagree agreeably" about Christ. I also wanted people to feel free *not* not accept Christ and *not* to join the church.

> *Whether you share from a printed page or from the epistle of your personal experience, the Holy Spirit can use you to point your friends to the Cross.*

Several times Jim stood before the class and gave this testimony: "Making a decision about Jesus Christ is the most important decision you will make in your life. I do not personally believe that Jesus is the Son of God or that He was raised from the dead." Of course Jim's remarks startled some people. But his blunt honesty helped potential members realize that we were serious about wanting them to make their decisions for Christ carefully.

Just before Christmas 1981 I received one of Jim's frequent letters. But this one was the best of all of them:

> Ron,
> Just a short but important note before a busy holiday. I am proud to say that after three years of careful consideration, I am ready to accept Jesus Christ as my personal Lord and Savior. You and Carol were the primary people who provided the daily assistance for me to grow into my decision. As I declared at your inquirers' classes, deciding about Christ is the most important decision I will ever make. I have come to my decision to accept Christ voluntarily, deliberately, carefully, and correctly.
>
> Thank you, Ron.
>
> Jim Bolin

Whether you share from a printed page or from the epistle of your personal experience, the Holy Spirit can use you to point your friends to the Cross.

CHAPTER 11
A Household Affair

"Men, what must I do to be saved?" They replied, "Believe in the Lord Jesus, and you will be saved—you and your household." Then they spoke the word of the Lord to him and to all the others in his house. Acts 16:30,31,32

Curt Baker, a friend who is also in the ministry, told me the interesting story about the first time he met his future wife's parents, Martin and Emma Schull. Carolyn had invited him to spend a weekend at her parents' home in South Bend, Indiana. Curt put on his best clothes and plastered every hair into place with Vitalis (this was in the old days before hair spray).

Upon his arrival Curt met Carolyn's mom in the kitchen and they had a nice conversation. Then Mr. Schull walked in. "Hello purty Curty! Good to meet ya," he bubbled. "Hey, it's great to talk to somebody eyeball to eyeball—not like those other tall galoots and gorillas Carolyn has been bringing home!" Curt's father-in-law continued to treat "purty Curty" like a long lost friend through the evening meal.

Curt was fairly new at witnessing, but after dinner he

began to share the gospel with Mr. and Mrs. Schull. As a pre-med student Curt knew something about the human anatomy. And the more he witnessed, the more Mr. Schull's anatomy changed. His face gradually flushed red

Most every Christian has an immediate family member or close relative who is in need of coming to know Jesus Christ.

and the veins in his neck and temples swelled and turned purple. And then Mr. Schull exploded! How dare this young wise guy talk about religion to them that way! He had no right!

Mr. Schull was correct; Curt *didn't* have the right to witness because he hadn't earned the right. He was a guest in their home and had only known them for a few hours. He was totally insensitive to the situation.

After a rocky start, a positive relationship developed between Curt and the Schulls, mainly because he became their son-in-law. It was 13 years after their first meeting that Curt's in-laws came to visit the church where he was preaching. His text was Philippians 2:12: "Therefore, my dear friends, as you have always obeyed—not only in my presence, but now much more in my absence— continue to work out your salvation with fear and trembling." The choir sang, "When I Survey the Wondrous Cross." From the beginning of the service until the end, Mr. and Mrs. Schull heard what salvation was all about and how they could enter into a personal relationship with the Lord.

After the service a tearful Mr. Schull came up to his son-in-law and hugged him. "Curt, we've known each other for 13 years," he said, "and we've had good times and bad times together. You were a real jerk for trying to push your religion on us the first day we met. I figured you were like a lot of ministers—you couldn't practice what you preached and you couldn't ask forgiveness for your mistakes. But over the years I've seen you make mistakes and I've heard your confessions. It's because you have really been a friend to me that today I was able to hear the gospel in a way I've never heard it before."

All in the Family

Most every Christian has an immediate family member or close relative who is in need of coming to know Jesus Christ. Yet it is often very difficult to witness to those we care about most. In these situations it is doubly crucial that we exercise the principles of FRIENDS evangelism.

The following outline is a guide for leading family members to Christ. Each letter in the words FAMILY MEMBERS represents a point of wisdom to consider:

Be a Family Friend

F—Find common ground with each family member because each individual is unique. If you really want to be a friend to your family members, you must learn to show an interest in the things each one does (see 1 Cor. 9:20,22).

A—Admit your errors, failures and inconsistencies in living the Christian life. Face it: Nobody knows your faults better than your family, so be real. Ask for forgiveness when you blow it (see Matt. 5:23,24).

M—Ask God to heal any bad **memories** you have of your family members. Ephesians 6:4 indicates that our parents are sometimes guilty of provoking anger in us. You may have some bad memories of an unjustly angry parent. Ask God to heal any bad memory in mind or spirit—recent or distant past—that might erect a barrier in a relationship with a family member.

I—Intercede for your family members. James 4:2 says that we do not *have* because we do not *ask*. There is good biblical grounds for praying for family members: Abraham prayed for Ishmael, Hannah for Samuel, David for Absalom and Andrew for Peter. Speak to God about your family, then speak to your family about God.

L—Love your family members as they are. You may not love what they do, but you must love them (see 1 Pet. 4:8; 1 Cor. 13). Expose family members to your love so they will be more open to the love of God. Stop trying to change them. Love them and let God change them. Allow God to love your family members through you.

Y—You must do your part if God is to do His part. You be the person to change and then watch your family members change. Reveal the changing power of Christ by letting your family see the change in you (see Matt. 7:1-5).

Special Benefits for Members

M—Mention the gospel in nonthreatening ways. Keep your ears open for opportunities to easily and naturally reveal spiritual tidbits through everyday conversations. Jesus did this when Nicodemus came to Him (see John 3:1-3). Each time you share the gospel you add another link in the chain leading your family members' salvation.

E—Explain the plan of salvation at some time. We need to ask God for a divine appointment, a time when we can speak sensitively to our family members about God's plan of salvation so that they will hear it clearly (see Rom. 10:17). You may use any of the methods outlined in the previous chapters for sharing the good news with family members.

M—Maintain your friendship with your family members. Often new Christians lose contact with non-Christians as they move into Christian relationships. But John 17:15-18 reminds us to stay in touch with non-Christians, including family members.

B—Believe God is at work in the lives of your family members. Philippians 1:6 says that God has begun a good work and will bring it to completion. Remember: God is the primary evangelist. He is even more interested in your loved ones coming to Christ than you are.

E—Express your love in words *and* actions. James 2:17 says that faith without works is dead. I say that *love* without words is dead. Say "I love you" frequently to your family members. But also express your love for them outwardly with hugs and loving deeds.

R—Remember the special days of their lives: birthdays, anniversaries and other occasions (see Deut. 32:7). Record these dates on your calendar to help you remember them. Then be sure to express your love with a phone call, card or gift.

S—Serve your family members. Remember the Son of Man came to serve others rather than to be served (see Mark 10:45). Be a servant in your attitude and in your deeds and watch what happens.

I have found these 13 suggestions to be most helpful in leading my own family members and relatives to a personal faith relationship with Jesus Christ. Sometimes it has been years before I have seen a response, but God has been faithful.

A Family Matter

Bruce and Barbara had been married for 10 years when

they learned that Barbara's popular little sister Bonnie had become pregnant the night of her junior prom. Bonnie decided to carry the child and finish high school, but she dreaded the months of public embarrassment in her rural Indiana home town. So she asked her parents if she could move to Cincinnati for her senior year. Arrangements were made with an organization that would provide Bonnie's room, board and medical care. Bonnie looked forward to being with her sister and brother-in-law on weekends.

Bruce and Barbara began taking Bonnie with them to church on Sunday mornings. At first Bonnie didn't want to go, but soon she realized that the church members accepted and encouraged her. She even became friends with several people her own age.

As Bonnie neared her delivery date her spirits drooped low. So one night Bruce took her out to dinner at a four-star French restaurant. They enjoyed a wonderful meal with excellent service in a beautiful setting. Bruce gave Bonnie a flower for her hair to help her feel loved and attractive—and she did.

As they drove home Bonnie talked about the love the church people had shown "even to someone like me." She expressed her gratitude that Bruce and Barbara had opened their home to her and loved her when she felt so terrible. And for the first time since she arrived in Cincinnati the tears began to flow.

Bruce and Barbara had talked to Bonnie about God's love many times, but this seemed to be a special opportunity. Bruce quoted Matthew 11:28 from the *King James Version*, "Come unto me, all ye that labour and are heavy laden, and I will give you rest." The verse seemed very appropriate since Bonnie would soon be in labor and since she was so heavy laden with shame. Bruce pulled the car to the side of the road and took Bonnie's hand. Together they prayed that the Lord would come into her heart and fill her with His love and joy.

After they prayed Bonnie suddenly exclaimed, "I am delivered! I am delivered!" Bruce thought she meant that she had started labor and was going to deliver the baby right there in his car! But she meant that she was delivered of the burden of guilt and shame that she had carried. They wept and hugged each other, thanking God for a very special time of deliverance.

A few weeks later Bonnie gave birth to a beautiful baby boy. Together Bruce, Bonnie and Barbara laid hands on the child and asked God to care for him and bless him as he went to his adoptive parents. Bonnie, Barbara and Bruce believe that somewhere in the world there is a child whom the Lord intends to use in a special way. They expect to meet that boy in heaven some day and discover how he has been used by the Lord because of their love and trust in God's goodness.

Barbara and Bonnie grew up in a Roman Catholic home and felt a special closeness to Mary the mother of Jesus. When Bonnie felt alone or condemned, she remembered that Mary too was unmarried and pregnant and in a position of public shame. And when Bonnie had to release her son into the hands of adoptive parents, Barbara helped her remember how Mary also released her Son into the hands of God.

Bringing the Children to Jesus

Tim and Linda Warner were both PKs (preacher's kids). Their son Martin had been baptized as an infant by both of his grandfathers.

Several years later Tim attended a FRIENDS evangelism seminar in which we discussed several methods for leading children to Christ. After attending the first session Tim was giving Martin a bath. Out of the blue the child said, "I want to know Jesus like you and Grandpa know Jesus." Tim could hardly believe his ears. A child's openness to his parents' faith was exactly what we had discussed in class! Tim stuttered and stammered, then helped his son pray a simple prayer of commitment as the boy sat in the bath water. Tim used the illustration of Jesus, the Living Water, who washes away our sin and gives us eternal life.

Childish Principles. There is a chapter in my book *For Fathers Who Aren't in Heaven* that specifically talks about leading our children to Christ. Virtually all of the methods of FRIENDS evangelism are simple enough to share with children, particularly the ABCs and some of the illustrated pamphlets. I firmly believe that if we expose our children to strong links—Sunday School teachers, camp leaders, faithful lay people and so on—and let them observe our own prayer and Bible reading at home, opportunities will arise for us to lead them to Christ. If we let them see us asking forgiveness for our faults and ministering to others in love, they will be open to asking forgiveness for their own sin and ready to come to Christ for salvation.

These concepts are based on Deuteronomy 6 and Joshua 4. In each passage parents were told how to respond when their children asked why questions about Israel's beliefs. If your life is a testimony of your faith, your children will inevitably ask about it. If a child asks "What does this holiday mean?" or "What did the Sunday School teacher mean?" or "Why did the pastor say such and such?" it is very natural for the parent to say, "My son or my daughter, they have been talking about their personal relationship with Jesus Christ. I would like very much for you to meet Jesus Christ, too."

Two for the Price of One

Libby is one of our church secretaries. She was tucking her two boys into their bunk beds one evening when her older son Glenn asked her to sit on his lower bunk and talk

> *Your faith may be weak, but God will meet you at the point of your need. Continue to ask Him to build your faith as you love your loved ones into the Kingdom.*

with him before she turned out the lights. He told her how he was having problems with bullies at school and that he hated one particular child who was mean to him. Libby talked with him about forgiveness and the need to love those who hurt him. Glenn said he just couldn't love the bullies. Libby told him how Jesus loved His enemies, even forgiving the soldiers who crucified Him. Glenn said he would try if Jesus would try! They prayed together asking Jesus to come into Glenn's heart and forgive him for his sins. Then Glenn asked that his anger and hurt be replaced with Jesus' love and peace.

The next morning Libby's mother stopped in for coffee and Libby's younger son Scotty ran in to give his grandmother a hug. "Guess what, Gramma!" he cried. "Glenn an' me have Jesus in our hearts now!"

Gramma asked how it had happened. Scotty said his mom had prayed with them when they went to bed the night before. "But Scotty," Libby interrupted, "I only prayed with Glenn. I thought you were already asleep."

"I know," he answered. "But I was only pretending. I prayed in secret when you prayed with Glenn, so now I have Jesus in my heart too!"

God says that His Word will not return to Him void. Sometimes we have no idea how potent His Word can be!

Pray and Believe

Remember the father who came to Jesus on behalf of his demon-possessed son?

> Jesus asked the boy's father, "How long has he been like this?"
> "From childhood," he answered . . . . "But if you can do anything, take pity on us and help us."
> "'If you can'?" said Jesus. "Everything is possible for him who believes."
> Immediately the boy's father exclaimed, "I do believe; help me overcome my unbelief!" (Mark 9:21-24).

Often we pray a similar prayer when we bring our unsaved loved ones to Christ. Your faith may be weak, but God will meet you at the point of your need. Continue to ask Him to build your faith as you love your loved ones into the Kingdom.

CHAPTER 12

Hear, O Israel

I am not ashamed of the gospel, because it is the power of God for the salvation of everyone who believes; first for the Jew, then for the Gentile. Romans 1:16

Most of us are not ashamed to admit that when it comes to witnessing to our Jewish friends we are in need of some help. This chapter applies the principles of FRIENDS evangelism to the unique spiritual characteristics of the Jewish people.

A *Shema* for Witnesses

Ancient Jews instituted the practice of reciting several verses of Scripture twice daily. The recited passage is found in Deuteronomy 6:4-9 and is known as the *shema*, meaning "hear." The verses begin with the words, "Hear, O Israel." I have used these three words as an acrostic to

help Christians witness effectively to their Jewish friends.
Like the *shema*, perhaps these principles should be recited
twice daily until they become ingrained in our thinking.

Becoming Jews to Win the Jews

H—The Christian needs to adopt a **humble** spirit
when witnessing to Jewish friends. Christianity has its
roots in Judaism. God revealed His grace to the Jews first,
and then secondarily to us Gentiles who are grafted into
vine (see Rom. 11:17-21). The recognition of the Jews'
central role in God's plan should cause us to approach
them with humility.

E—The Christian needs to express **empathy** toward
Jewish friends. Empathy is the projection of one's personality into the personality of another in order to understand
him or her better. In 1 Corinthians 9:20 Paul said, "To the
Jews I became like a Jew, to win the Jews." We must do no
less if we are to win our Jewish friends.

> *We must realize that the most important
> thing to our Jewish friends is remaining a
> Jew no matter what. Therefore if we are
> going to present Christ to our Jewish
> friends, we must present Him in a Jewish
> context—*

If we are to "become like a Jew" we must realize that
the most important thing to our Jewish friends is remaining
a Jew no matter what. Therefore if we are going to
present Christ to our Jewish friends, we must present
Him in a Jewish context—otherwise it would not be
kosher! Witnessing in a Jewish context is not difficult.
After all, Jesus was Jewish, His disciples were Jewish, the

first believers were Jewish and the writers of the Scriptures were Jewish.

A—We need to **ask** God's Spirit to remove the hardness of heart which characterizes our Jewish friends (see Rom. 11:25). God is the evangelist who can break through barriers and draw people to Himself.

R—We must **reflect** upon Jewish history and what Christianity has meant to the Jews. Bear these facts in mind:

- The Crusades were a source of great persecution of Jews as well as the Moslems. Many Jews were killed in the name of Christ.
- The Inquisitions (Spanish, Portuguese, French and German) were a means of forced conversions to Christianity. Jewish people faced deportation from their homeland if they did not convert to Christianity.
- Germany, which the Jews looked upon as a Christian nation, produced Hitler, the Nazis and the attempted annihilation of the Jews.

The Old Foundation

O—The **Old Testament**, which Jews accept as God's Word, must be the foundation for witnessing to Jewish friends. Interestingly, everything which needs to be revealed about Jesus the Messiah is found in the Old Testament.

The Story of the Suffering Servant

I—We need to indicate openly our **indebtedness** to the Jews and their heritage for God's plan of salvation. You can say something like: "I am indebted to the Jewish people and their heritage for through them I have come to know the God of Abraham, Isaac and Jacob." When you are indebted to someone, two important communication factors begin to operate. The witness exudes an attitude of warmth, empathy and respect, while the person being witnessed to takes on an attitude of warmth, openness and receptivity.

> *Isaiah 53 is probably the most powerful passage of Scripture you can use in witnessing to Jewish friends.*

S—Sketch out the unique story of salvation from the Old Testament. This story has as its theme three covenants between God and mankind. These covenants can be remembered from the letters ABC:

- *A—The Abrahamic Covenant:* God's first covenant was with Abraham (see Gen. 17:4-7). In this covenant, God joined Himself to Abraham personally, established him as the father of all nations, revealed that from him would come kings and committed Himself to be his God and the God of his descendants. Abraham is the seed, Israel is the root and all the descendants are the fruit of this covenant. This covenant is important because it establishes the origin and source of the Jewish people. The sign of this covenant is circumcision. The key to the covenant is Abraham's faith in the promise of God.
- *B—The Blood Covenant:* The blood covenant is established in Leviticus 16 and 17 and centers on atonement, which simply means

becoming "at-one" with God (see Lev. 16:29,30,34). The blood covenant states that atonement for sin and the souls of mankind is available only through the sacrifices of life or blood. In the Old Testament God covenanted (agreed) to cover the sins of His people through a sacrificial system. The sign of this covenant is the blood of an animal and the key again is faith. The people believed that their sins were covered.

The blood covenant is incomplete for two reasons: (1) it did not *remove* sin, only *covered* it; and (2) it had to be repeated annually. It therefore looked forward in faith to a final and perfect sacrifice.

- *C—The Completed Covenant:* The completed covenant describes the promised sacrifice of God—the Messiah—who did not cover the sins of mankind, but took them upon Himself and became the offering for sin (see Isa. 53:4-6,10). Isaiah 53 is probably the most powerful passage of Scripture you can use in witnessing to Jewish friends.

The sign of this covenant is the Suffering Servant. The key is faith in Him and what He has accomplished on behalf of all. Who is the Suffering Servant of Isaiah 53? Jews will often answer that the description represents either the prophets or the nation of Israel. Neither of these answers are adequate because neither the prophets nor Israel as a nation were sinless. Furthermore, neither of these entities claimed to take away sin as described in Isaiah 53.

R—Raise the question: "Who do you say the Suffering Servant is?"

A—Answer the question yourself, but by all means avoid using the following Christian terms:

- *"Jew"* or *"Jews"*: It is better to use the phrase "the Jewish people."
- *"Christian"* or *"Christianity"*: Though "Christian" literally means "a follower of the Christ, the Messiah," its meaning is tainted for Jewish people because of its historical context, as discussed earlier.
- *"Do you desire to become a Christian?"*: This question is the equivalent to asking a Jew to disown his Jewish heritage and become a Gentile. The Jewish mind conceives of only two basic categories—Jew and Gentile (including Christian).
- *"Christ"* or *"Jesus"*: These titles are automatically associated with Christianity. Instead, use the title "Messiah Yeshua."
- *"Church"*: This term is also associated with Christianity since Jewish people do not worship in churches.
- *"Convert"*: Again, you are asking someone to change his nationality and religion. The Jewish people don't need to be converted, simply completed by accepting Yeshua as the Messiah.
- *"Baptism"*: A sure sign of conversion or the seal of Christianity to the Jewish person.
- *"Witnessing"*: This conjures up associations with the Jehovah Witnesses.
- *"Communion"* or *"Lord's Supper"*: Instead,

refer to these as the Passover Dinner or the New Covenant Passover.

- *"Original Sin"* and *"Virgin Birth"*: These are associated with Catholicism and therefore with Christianity.
- *"The Trinity"*: This term is erroneously associated with the worship of three gods rather than one God. Jewish people are fiercely monotheistic.
- *"The deity of Jesus"*: This phrase is often associated with Catholicism and the worship of idols, statues or pictures.

When witnessing to the Jewish person, the question, "Who is the Suffering Servant?" must be answered without using Christian jargon. You can simply say, "I believe Isaiah is describing the Messiah, and in particular, 'Yeshua of Nazareth.'"

E—Explain God's plan of salvation through Messiah Yeshua, as revealed in the three covenants, using such Jewish terms as:

- *"Yeshua"*: Jesus in Hebrew.
- *"Messiah*: The Anointed One.
- *"Messianic"*: A follower of the Messiah Yeshua.
- *"Messianic Judaism," "Completed Jew"* or *"Fulfilled Jew"*: Judaism which has by faith accepted Yeshua as the Messiah.
- *"Would you like to complete yourself in the Messiah?"* or *"Would you like to fulfill yourself by putting your faith in Yeshua as the Messiah?"*.
- *"Sharing the Messiah"*: Instead of "witnessing."

The Old Testament contains some 60 major prophecies that are fulfilled in Yeshua. In these prophecies, God identifies the Messiah and separates Him from all other men of God. For example, in Micah 5:2 God revealed the exact city where the Messiah would be born. And in Genesis 3:15 God revealed that the Messiah would come from the seed of woman. Every other Jewish person is traced from the seed of man. Yet Messiah would also be of the house of David.

For further help on messianic prophecies, a special prophecy New Testament is available through the Messianic Jewish Movement International, 7315 Wisconsin Avenue, Washington, D.C. 20014. The booklet entitled *Christ in Every Book in the Bible*, by Oral Roberts (Pinoak Publications, Tulsa, OK) is also an excellent tool to use for seeing Yeshua proclaimed in the Old Testament.

Another important tool to help you explain God's plan of salvation is the booklet titled, *Have You Heard of the Five Jewish Laws*, also published by the Messianic Jewish Movement International. Another resource organization is the American Messianic Fellowship, 7448 North Damen Avenue, Chicago, IL 60645.

L—Lead your Jewish friends with love and sensitivity to accept Messiah Yeshua by personal faith. Emphasize that one becomes a fulfilled or completed Jew when he or she places faith in the Messiah Yeshua. Invite your Jewish friends to pray an ABC prayer of commitment: Yeshua, I *acknowledge* that you are the promised Messiah. I *believe* in you as my personal atonement. I now *covenant* with you to be your follower.

The Importance of Sensitivity

The guidelines presented above for sharing the good news

with Jewish friends underscore the importance of sensitivity in all our witnessing efforts. Insensitivity to others violates the very foundation of FRIENDS evangelism—winning the right to be heard. We are insensitive witnesses when we coldly and thoughtlessly express the gospel with our lips without seeking to find common ground, reveal Christ through our lives and intercede for our friends. An experience of my friend Tom Jennings, the car dealer we met in chapter 1, will illustrate the point.

After Tom came to know Jesus Christ he began to make Jesus the Lord of every aspect of his life, including his automobile dealership. In addition to hosting a Bible study and prayer time each week, Tom also placed a New Testament in the glove compartment of each new and used car sold at his dealership. After all, the auto maker included an owner's manual with each new car, providing instructions on how to correctly care for every aspect of the vehicle. As a Christian, Tom wanted to give each customer a copy of the "manufacturer's manual" containing instructions on how to correctly care for every aspect of life. This is the letter Tom included with each car and New Testament:

> Dear Customer: I want to thank you for placing your trust and confidence in Jennings Buick for your automobile needs. This book is a gift from me to you. Just as your new car owners' manual explains how your new car operates, God's Word (the Bible) explains how His plan and order for our lives works. This paraphrased version of the New Testament written in today's language has helped to simplify the deep and often complex thoughts of the Word of God for me. It is my hope that you will discover His

plan for your life just as I have by looking up the answers to the questions on page 5 in the very front.

Sincerely,
Tom Jennings, President

Some weeks after Tom began this new practice, a couple of his salespeople came to speak with him in his office. They said they respected Tom's personal beliefs, but they felt they could not in good conscience give the testimony letter and New Testament to their customers. The Bible study was different because employees could attend or not attend as they pleased. But the New Testaments were placed in *all* the cars regardless of the salesperson's personal faith. They felt it was improper to impose one's religious belief on others.

There are times when we make mistakes in our witnessing and offend others by our method, style or plain old insensitivity.

Tom saw that his employees were right. He thanked them for coming to him personally and speaking frankly, and he sincerely asked their forgiveness. The New Testaments and testimony letters were removed from the glove compartments of the cars and were instead made available to customers from a desk in the showroom.

There are times when we make mistakes in our witnessing and offend others by our method, style or plain old insensitivity. We may assume that a friend is not a Christian because he or she does not use evangelical jargon or because he is private and quiet about matters of faith. Or we may try to speak about repentance and salvation at a time when our friend really needs personal comfort and encouragement. Or we may approach with judgment when the need is for grace. True, the gospel itself will offend people. But we should not think that the gospel's offense grants us license to be offensive.

In Matthew 5:23,24 we are instructed: "Therefore, if you are offering your gift at the altar and there remember that your brother has something against you, leave your gift there in front of the altar. First go and be reconciled to your brother; then come and offer your gift." We must be alert to those occasions when we offend our non-Christians by our words, deeds or attitudes. When the Holy Spirit points out to us that we have offended someone, or when the offended person or a friend of the offended person tells us that we have blundered, we must go to the person we have offended and try to be reconciled.

When confessing a personal failure to a non-Christian friend, it is always best to use "I" and "me" pronouns instead of the accusatory "you." This allows us to recognize, own and admit our part in a clumsy witnessing experience and keeps us from putting the offended friend on the defensive. In speaking to the offended friend, say something like: "I have come to realize that I was insensitive in the manner in which I approached you. Will you please forgive me for my insensitivity?"

The words "will you forgive me" will minister to the spirit of the friend who has been offended. These words should be used together with the words "I was insensitive" or "I was wrong" in preference to the words "I am sorry." You can be intellectually sorry for a situation and still have a haughty spirit instead of a humble spirit. The thief may be very sincerely sorry that he got caught, but he may not be convinced that he was wrong.

When you confess your insensitivity, the offended friend usually becomes much more open to hearing the truth of the gospel because you have demonstrated the gospel through your confession. Jesus said, "You will know the truth, and the truth will set you free" (John 8:32). In this case, the truth sets the offender and the offended free from the past experience. If the offended friend does not choose to forgive you, continue to express an attitude of love and acceptance.

Out Of Sight, Out Of Mind

Bobby Bradford was instrumental in leading his friend Ted Hartman to the Lord. Ted had been an alcoholic for most of his life. Through many months of deep caring and support from Bobby, Ted went "on the wagon" and became active in the fellowship at Bobby's church.

As time went on, Ted became involved in different committees and activities and Bobby didn't see him as often as before. Then Bobby noticed that Ted was absent from services on Sundays and Wednesday nights. He knew that he ought to stop by Ted's house and see how he was doing, but he put it off. A few weeks went by and Bobby intended to phone Ted, but put it off again.

It was six months later when Bobby saw Ted in the narthex at church one Sunday. Bobby immediately approached Ted and put his arm around him. "We need to get together, friend. I haven't seen you for so long."

But Ted was not smiling. "I'm ashamed of you, Bobby," Ted said, obviously wounded. "I'm ashamed of you and this church. I've been through six months of misery and nobody even cared enough to find out where I was!"

"You're right," Bobby admitted soberly. "I was insensitive and I didn't take time to do what I knew needed to be done. I need your forgiveness."

That week Bobby and Ted were reconciled through confession, gentle rebuke and forgiveness. Bobby shared his experience with the pastor and others at church, persons who knew Ted and who might have noticed his absence and reached out to him. Through this failure the church learned a valuable lesson on the need for sensitivity, faithfulness and forgiveness.

Hopefully we can learn the same lesson before we insensitively offend the Jewish friends, customers, co-workers and Teds in our lives.

CHAPTER 13
Catch the Vision

*The things you have heard me say in the
presence of many witnesses entrust to
reliable men who will also be qualified to
teach others.* 2 Timothy 2:2

Our home is the frequent gathering place for groups of
people from our church, and our driveway and street often
resemble a crowded parking lot. One Sunday evening
there were several church people meeting in our home
when suddenly we heard the screeching of tires and a
grinding *crunch, crunch, crunch* out front. We ran outside
to find a shaken young man climbing out of a smashed car
on my lawn. He had been driving too fast and lost control,
slamming into three of the cars parked in front of our
house before skidding onto our lawn.

While Jennifer called the police our church members
ministered to the young man named Gary. The police
arrived and were puzzled that the owners of the damaged
cars—Janet, Bill and Bob—were not angry. Gary's parents arrived soon afterward and they too were surprised
and even embarrassed because we were so understanding
and loving toward their son.

On Tuesday evening Janet, Bill and Bob went to visit

Gary and his family. Their friendly attitude about the accident opened the door for them to share the gospel with Gary and his mother. Gary made a commitment to Christ and his mother recommitted her life to the Lord.

As they talked, our members learned that Gary had recently been hired at a fast-food restaurant that was operated by a another member of our congregation named John Mattis. In the following weeks Janet, Bill and Bob made additional visits to Gary's home. Meanwhile Gary and his mother began attending church regularly, and Gary continually received encouragement and affirmation from his boss John.

When Gary's car swerved out of control that Sunday night, he had no idea that he would "run into" a group of people that God had prepared to change his life. But the fact that Janet, Bill and Bob were ready to love Gary and bring him to Christ was certainly no "accident."

A Church Full of Evangelists

How would you feel if every member of your church—including yourself—was as ready, willing and able to share Christ with others as Janet, Bill and Bob were? It's unlikely that 100 percent of your church members will become FRIENDS evangelists. But think what could happen in your community if 25, 50 or 75 percent of your congregation was trained in FRIENDS evangelism principles and just waiting to "bump into" people like Gary.

The primary goal of this book is to equip individual Christians with a variety of ways to express their faith to their friends through the principles of FRIENDS evangelism. But why not expand this concept, as we do at College Hill Presbyterian Church, to include the equipping of an entire congregation for evangelism? It will take some time and effort to implement evangelism training on a churchwide scale, but the results will easily outweigh the expense.

It will take some time and effort to implement evangelism training on a churchwide scale, but the results will easily outweigh the expense.

Dr. C. Peter Wagner of Fuller Theological Seminary notes that if church leaders are serious about evangelism and growth, they must equip church members—especially new members—with formal training for sharing their faith. He also suggests that most churches are not involved in large-scale evangelism training because pastors and church boards are too timid. Wow! That's a challenge!

I wonder if you as an individual are willing to consider accepting the challenge to become an instrument of change in your congregation. Consider becoming a reliable witness who will also be qualified to teach others to witness. "Who me?" you say? Yes you! Why not? Others have caught the vision; why not you? Remember: "God did not give us a spirit of timidity, but a spirit of power, of love and of self-discipline" (2 Tim. 1:7).

Meet and Prepare

The following outline, an acrostic based on the key phrase MEET AND PREPARE, supplies a practical means for introducing churchwide FRIENDS evangelism to your congregation. I have recommended this plan of action to numerous

pastors and lay persons who have accepted the 2 Timothy
2:2 challenge for their congregations.

Laying the Groundwork

M—Meet with your pastor if you are a lay person or
with some of your lay leadership if you are a pastor.

E—Explain your vision for equipping your entire
congregation in FRIENDS evangelism principles and methods. Explain how FRIENDS evangelism can be a natural
means of church growth. Explain your perception of the
need and the opportunity for churchwide evangelism.
Share copies of this book with them and suggest that you
meet again after each individual has read and studied the
book.

E—Explore the various options for this vision to
become a reality in your congregation. For example, discuss the schedule options for conducting training classes in
your church: Sunday mornings, Sunday evenings, mid-
week, breakfasts, luncheons, home group meetings, etc.
Think creatively and explore a variety of possible solutions.

T—Take a proposal to the official board of leaders in
your church. Meet with them to explain your vision and to
explore with them the options for a systematic approach to
equipping your members to reveal their faith to their
friends.

I emphasize the importance of meeting with your pastor and ruling board first so the training ministry involves
the whole church from the beginning. If there is resistance
or disagreement, take time to explain FRIENDS evangelism
sensitively and patiently to those who express concerns.
Cutting corners and risking misunderstanding or wounded
feelings can doom the ministry to failure before it starts.
Patiently and respectfully work through the proper chan-

nels to achieve agreement from your ruling board for the general FRIENDS evangelism goals.

Proposing a Plan

A—Ask permission from the board of leaders to experiment with a pilot series of FRIENDS classes. Suggesting an experiment communicates openness, evaluation, flexibility and process instead of a final decision which is set in concrete. You are asking for permission to experiment with an idea in order to discover if the vision can become a reality.

N—Inform board members that you will **notify** them regularly about the progress and results of the experiment. Communication is vital. The board needs to feel that they are included and well-informed in order to assume personal ownership of the proposed experiment or project.

D—Develop a game plan for implementing your experiment to equip church members in FRIENDS evangelism principles. The game plan should include the following (based on the acrostic GAME):

- *G—Goals:* Several clear, specific statements that describe the intended outcome of the experiment.
- *A—Action Steps:* Several specific behavioral or performance statements that describe how the goals will be accomplished.
- *M—Measurements:* Statements for determining the effectiveness and accomplishment of the action steps. For example: By the end of the experiment we will have trained 10 church members how to use the ABCs of Christianity.

- *E—Evaluations:* Specific statements that identify the strengths and weaknesses of the completed experiment. Proper evaluation leads to specific recommendations for the future.

Putting the Plan in Gear

P—Pick those who will lead and implement the training. Pick dates and times for training, pick places where the training will occur and pick individuals, organizations or groups from the congregation to be a part of this experiment. Since you have read this book and have sought to implement FRIENDS evangelism in your own life, be willing to serve as a leader and equipper of others.

R—Recruit the persons and groups you have selected. Recruitment may be done by the pastor or other leaders through bulletin announcements, letters or meetings. A special recruitment meeting can be helpful for gathering all interested persons to discuss the proposed training project.

E—Explain the vision to the recruits. Outline its history and its proposed effect on the life of the congregation. Answer all the questions posed by the recruits. Extend an invitation to each recruit to become a part of the training experiment. Those who respond positively will form the core group.

P—Prepare the core group to reveal their faith in Jesus Christ through the training schedule you have determined. Get ready to implement your game plan using the people God has given you.

A—Announce to the congregation what is taking place in the training sessions. Announcements may consist of information presented by the pastors and testimonies from those who have benefitted from the training. We frequently ask lay persons to prepare and present three-minute testimonies to the congregation on a wide range of themes, including evangelism. These presentations have had a powerful, encouraging and upbuilding effect on our congregation. Announcements and testimonies about the training experiment help prepare the entire congregation to consider becoming part of the training emphasis in the future.

R—After the core group has tried the experiment they should meet with the leaders to **reveal** the results and **recommend** that the ministry be continued (or discontinued). It is my experience and observation that this evaluation report will result in the leaders' enthusiastic support for the ministry.

E—**After completing the successful experiment and receiving the green light to continue, equip** other church members to evangelize their friends. Use the original core group and those who attended the pilot classes to train others in Friends evangelism. This is the 2 Timothy 2:2 principle in action: equipping some who in turn can equip others and so build up the Body of Christ.

The Game Plan at College Hill

We have followed an effective evangelism training game plan at College Hill Presbyterian Church for several years. Our game plan is comprised of three parts.

The first part is an all-day Saturday Friends evangelism training session for all persons enrolled in the new members class. These training sessions are held twice a year during the third week of the 10-week new members series. The sessions are also open to church members who may have missed part or all of the training earlier or who wish to brush up on their witnessing skills.

During the Saturday training session we teach most of the witnessing methods presented in this book. We also form teams of two to practice the methods and to pray for one another for 30 days following the training.

Participants are asked to practice one witnessing method per week for the seven remaining weeks of the new members class. They may practice on Christian friends or family members, or on a friend who may not be Christian. The purpose of this required practice schedule is to acquaint individuals with a variety of methods so each person can discover at least one method he or she is comfortable with. Each week we have members fill out a simple report card evaluating their practice experience.

The second part of our game plan is the HELPER seminar, a series of evangelism training classes lasting up to 10 weeks. HELPER seminars are offered several times during the year in a variety of time slots to meet the schedules of our members. We usually teach one witnessing method per week which share-prayer pairs practice together. These training classes are now quite small since 75 percent of the over 2,200 persons attending our church have become church members and have completed their evangelism training.

The third part of our game plan is the FRIENDS evangelism training series on video and audiocassette tape. We encourage the many small groups in our church to use the training series as part of their small group experience. Each group determines its own game plan for using the tapes.

I challenge you! Dr. C. Peter Wagner challenges you! Catch the vision! Meet and prepare! As Joshua said to the people of Israel overlooking the Promised Land: "Prepare provisions for yourselves . . . to go in to possess the land which the LORD your God is giving you" (Josh. 1:11, *NASB*).

Tips from Other Travelers

When you are about to embark on a long automobile trip, it is helpful to obtain good information about the road you plan to travel. A map can help you discover distances between towns and interesting side trips and attractions. A call to the highway department may reveal important

> *Expect frustration; thank God for His perseverance; keep trusting and being a friend.*

weather information, road conditions and possible traffic problems along the way. But perhaps the best information can be obtained from a friend who has just completed the same trip and who calls or writes to offer helpful, knowledgeable tips for your journey.

During our years of experience with FRIENDS evangelism at College Hill Presbyterian Church we have gathered a lot of helpful data about churchwide evangelism ministry. As you anticipate a journey on the same highway, allow these tidbits of information to help you know what to expect along the way.

Information. Knowing the Scriptures and understanding a variety of methods are very important to an evangelism ministry. This book and others recommended in the Appendix are excellent resources for biblical evangelism rationale and methods. But don't put off active witnessing until you feel that you know everything you need to know. I have been witnessing and training people to witness since 1967, and I still don't know all I need to know. The most usable information on evangelism will be obtained as you actually participate in sharing the good news with your friends and neighbors.

Frustration. Most people experience periods of frustration in the ministry of sharing the gospel with their friends. Some are frustrated by the volume of information—Scripture verses and methods—they are asked to learn. Others are frustrated after interceding for their friends for a long period of time without the doors opening for them to express their faith verbally. Expect frustration; thank God for His perseverance; keep trusting and being a friend.

Practice. There must be practice and experimentation in FRIENDS evangelism training. The "use it or lose it" and "practice makes perfect" principles apply here. Witnessing skills are more easily caught than taught. This is why we actually practice the methods in our training sessions and seminars as we teach them. People need to experience these principles in simulated witnessing situations.

Adaptation. Any and all of the methods, materials and insights presented in this book must be adapted to your own situation. Please don't take this material verbatim and transplant it directly into your church setting without filtering it through your denominational, ethnic and cultural distinctives.

A pastor wrote to me after attending one of our FRIENDS seminars. He recommended the training enthusiastically, but also said: "Do I as a pastor have any reservations? Sure I do. Some of the 'theology' communicated came in forms that are not entirely comfortable to me.

However, the seminar leaders expect that . . . I will be doing a bit of adapting."

I once saw a newspaper article on fishing which caught my attention. It listed a number of good fishing spots and described what kind of bait was catching the most fish in each area. The list looked like this:

Cowan Lake—Bluegill biting on red worms.
Grayton—Bluegill fair on worms in bays.
Fishtrap—Bluegill good on crickets in inlets.
Herrington—Bluegill good on worms along deep banks.
Kentucky—Bluegill good along shallow banks.
Buckhorn—Bluegill good on catalpa worms.

The article made me think of Jesus' approach to Andrew and Peter: "Come, follow me . . . and I will make you fishers of men" (Matt. 4:19). Just as a good fisherman adapts his bait to the kind of fish he wants to catch in a certain location, so we need to adapt our witnessing methods to the type of people we are seeking to reach. For example, a "fishers of folk" forecast might look like this:

Oxford—Students biting on pamphlets.
Downtown—Executives fair on personal testimony.
Greenhills—Yuppies good on abundant life.
Ridgelawn—Singles good on Romans Invitation.

Different methods are effective with different people. And even among people who have a lot in common, different methods will be effective at different times. So, fishers of folk, be equipped with a variety of methods and

198 Won by One

approaches so you can catch the fish when they're biting!

Implementation. Once a man reportedly criticized Billy Sunday for his method of evangelism. Mr. Sunday agreed that his method was not perfect, then he asked his critic how many persons he had led to Jesus Christ. The man answered none, so Billy Sunday said he would stick to his imperfect method.

The methods described in this book have been tried

> *Jesus Christ is the Lord of the harvest. God is the evangelist. The Holy Spirit is the one who will lead us in all we do. If we make ourselves available to Him, and if we prepare ourselves with appropriate methods and tools, we can depend on Him to use us to bring His good work to full fruition.*

and tested individually and corporately in tiny rural congregations and in major urban and suburban churches. They have been effective with highly educated persons as well as totally uneducated persons. They have crossed cultural, continental and language barriers. They are effective because they are simple. Everyone in the world needs a friend. And every Christian can be a friend by sharing Christ using the tools of FRIENDS evangelism.

Unless you are already seeing desired results with the method you are currently using, put the principles of FRIENDS evangelism into practice. They work!

Jesus Christ is the Lord of the harvest. God is the evangelist. The Holy Spirit is the one who will lead us in all we do. If we make ourselves available to Him, and if we prepare ourselves with appropriate methods and tools, we can depend on Him to use us to bring His good work to full fruition.

My prayer for each of you is that the impetus of Jesus' command to His original disciples will also motivate you to prayerful evangelistic ministry:

> All authority in heaven and on earth has been given to me. Therefore go and make disciples of all nations, baptizing them in the name of the Father and of the Son and of the Holy Spirit, and teaching them to obey everything I have commanded you. And surely I will be with you always, to the very end of the age (Matt. 28:18-20).

I also pray that you may be able to testify in the words of Paul concerning your involvement with your friends: "I have become all things to all men so that by all possible means I might save some. I do all this for the sake of the gospel, that I may share in its blessings" (1 Cor. 9:22,23).

Extra Witnessing Helps

This appendix contains a potpourri of my favorite examples, illustrations and techniques for witnessing. These helps can be used in conjunction with any of the methods presented in this book.

The appendix concludes with a section called Sources and Resources, a list of helpful pamphlets, tracts and books for witnessing.

Conversation Starters

As you find common ground with your friends, reveal your faith through your life and intercede for them, you look for opportunities to express your faith through your lips. But when those opportunities arise, how do you actually initiate a conversation about spiritual matters with a friend? Here are a few conversation starters that may be helpful. Notice that some questions deal with religious background, personal belief, the Bible and Christian symbols.

- Are you presently attending or involved with any particular church or synagogue? Why or why not?
- What is your family's religious preference or background? Do you agree with their preference? Why or why not?
- Are you finding that your religion is meaningful to you? Why or why not?
- What do you believe happens to a person when he or she dies? Do you believe in life after death? Why or why not?
- Why do you believe the Bible was written? What do you understand to be the purpose of the Bible?
- From your understanding and experience with churches, what would you say is the Church's purpose?
- Have your beliefs about God changed over the years? If so, how?
- What must a person do to get into heaven? If you came before God and He asked you, "Why should I allow you to enter my Kingdom?" what would you say?
- Who do you understand Jesus Christ to be?
- Why do you think we are here on this earth? What is your opinion of our reason for being?
- You know friend, as long as I've known you I don't think I've ever shared with you anything about my faith in God. May I share something about that with you?
- Friend, I would like to invite you to attend my church with me sometime. Would you be open to doing that?
- Friend, I have a lot of questions and problems

too. I have found some answers and solutions to them in the Bible. May I share some of these thoughts with you?

- What do you think about when you see a cross? (You may give your friend a small cross as you ask.)
- Why do you think the Bible is the world's all-time best-seller? Why does the Bible mean so much to so many people? What does the Bible mean to you? (You may present a gift Bible to your friend as you ask.)

The key to starting a conversation about the gospel is to listen and respond to our friends' questions, comments and problems. As we win the right to be heard, our friends will often provide the appropriate conversation starters concerning spiritual matters. Our primary task is to be ready to respond when the time is right (see 1 Pet. 3:15).

Four Ways to Pray

After I explained the good news about Jesus Christ to my wife-to-be, Jennifer looked at me with adoring eyes expecting me to lead her in a prayer of commitment. But I didn't know what to do! So we got in my car and drove to the church that I was attending. I took Jennifer into the empty church office and told her I would wait in the car while she spent some time alone in prayer. So I shut the door and waited. About 10 minutes later Jennifer came out, having accepted Jesus into her heart.

My passive, indirect prayer method worked fine on that occasion, but it would be rather impractical in most situations. Here are four basic ways to lead a friend in a prayer of commitment to Jesus Christ. They are listed in the order of my preference, but each of them is acceptable:

- You encourage your friend to pray the prayer out loud as you pray silently.
- You pray out loud and ask your friend to repeat the prayer out loud phrase by phrase after you.
- You pray out loud and ask your friend to pray silently.
- You both pray silently and you ask your friend to say amen when finished.

Perhaps the simplest and most direct prayer of commitment is the ABC prayer mentioned in previous chapters: Father, I *accept* your invitation. I *believe* in you for the forgiveness of my sins. I now *come* to you through faith in Jesus Christ. After your friend has prayed this prayer, you may desire to offer a brief prayer of thanksgiving.

Illustrations of Faith

While hiking in the Grand Canyon in 1987, I realized how much the human body needs water. The trail guide and my hiking books instructed me clearly to pack plenty of water. Throughout my long hike in that desert environment I continually perspired my body water content away. In order to maintain a healthy metabolism I had to assimilate water continually into my system. Our bodies are approximately 70 percent water and we must retain a certain water level or die.

For Christians, to believe—to have faith—means to

assimilate the very life of God in Christ into our souls and our experience. We must actually open our innermost beings to receive Him. Like our physical need for water, we need to renew the Spirit of Christ in us daily through prayer. In short, to believe in Christ means to have Him within us every moment.

The following illustrations provide simple, concrete and sometimes humorous explanations for faith:

The Airplane. Most people believe that airplanes can fly. But there are some people who *say* they believe in airplanes, but who won't get on a plane. They fear flying and would rather spend much more travel time on a bus or train than to trust their lives to an airplane.

If I mentally agree that airplanes can fly, but refuse to trust an airplane to fly me, I show that I do not truly believe in airplanes. I am only exercising true faith in an airplane when I buy a ticket, board the airplane and fly to my destination. Similarly, faith in Christ means more than simply agreeing that He can save those who come to Him. Even the devils have that kind of faith (see Jas. 2:19). True faith in Christ involves a total commitment to Him.

Blondin the Tightrope Walker. In 1857 a tightrope walker named Blondin stretched a two-inch steel cable across the gorge of Niagara Falls, attracting a large crowd. He said to the onlookers, "How many of you believe that I can carry the weight of a man on my shoulders across this gorge?" The crowd shouted and cheered their belief that he could do it. Sure enough, Blondin picked up a sack of sand weighing about 180 pounds and carried it across the falls.

Then Blondin said, "How many of you believe that I can actually carry a person across the gorge?" Many people in the crowd indicated that they thought he could do it. But then Blondin called out, "Which one of you will climb on my shoulders and let me carry you across the falls?"

Suddenly there was silence. Everyone wanted to see Blondin carry a person across the gorge and many believed he could. But nobody wanted to put his life in Blondin's hands.

Some time later Blondin did carry a man across Niagara Falls. The man was Blondin's manager, who had known the tightrope walker personally for many years. "You must not trust your own feelings, but mine," Blondin told his manager as they prepared for the crossing. "You will feel like turning when we don't need to turn. And if you trust your feelings we will both fall. You must become a part of me."

This is what faith in Jesus is: knowing Him personally and entrusting our eternal life into His hands (see John 15:4,5).

The Chicken and the Pig. Once upon a time a chicken and a pig lived in the same barnyard. One day they heard about a nearby orphanage in need of food. The children were hungry and the orphanage had no money.

The chicken said, "Brother Pig, why don't we go down to the orphanage and donate some food to those children? We could offer them a good ham-and-eggs breakfast."

"Wait a minute, Sister Chicken," the pig replied. "For you a ham-and-eggs breakfast may be just a donation. But for me it's a total commitment!"

Faith is not giving *something* to God, it's giving *someone* to God—yourself.

The Chair. I have often used a simple chair to illustrate faith, explaining: "Here is a chair. I believe in my mind that this is a chair because I have some knowledge about what chairs look like. But right now I'm not putting my faith in that chair. Even though I believe that it will support my weight, why can't I say for certain that it will indeed support my weight? Obviously because I'm not sitting on it! When I physically sit on the chair I express my confidence and faith in it."

Faith in Christ is similar. We need to know some facts about Him—that's mental belief. But the kind of faith described in the Bible is belief that acts upon what is known. It is not enough to believe in my mind that Christ can redeem me, I must act upon that fact.

Repelling. In the summer of 1986 my son Joshua and I went climbing in the Colorado mountains with a friend who is an expert climber. We worked our way up into the cliffs and then it was time to go down— straight down. I went first and discovered that repelling 100 feet was exciting, not fearful at all.

Then I looked up and saw Joshua beginning his descent. Suddenly I felt knots of fear in the pit of my stomach imagining all the things which could go wrong. As a father I realized that it was harder for me to trust the cord to lower my son than to trust it to lower me. Faith is like that too: letting yourself go over the edge with nothing to hold onto but a thin cord and the promise that someone above you won't let you go.

Illustrations of the Christian Life

In the course of leading your friend to Christ you may want to discuss with him or her some of the characteristics of the Christian life. Use the following illustrations to help your friends visualize some key principles.

The Dollar and the Watch. For this illustration you will need a Bible or New Testament, a dollar bill and a watch. Say something like: "Allow me to illustrate the importance of receiving Jesus Christ and the results of that decision. Jesus said that He came to give us abundant life in the present and eternal life in the future. Let this dollar bill represent abundant life in Christ and let this watch represent eternal life. We'll put the dollar and the watch into the New Testament (close the New Testament with the dollar bill and the watch inside).

"In order to receive the dollar bill and the watch, you need to receive the New Testament for they are contained in it. Similarly, in order to receive the abundant life and eternal life Jesus Christ offers, we must receive Him. The emphasis therefore is not on receiving the benefits Jesus brings, but on receiving Jesus.

"The Bible says: 'He came to that which was his own, but his own did not receive him. Yet to all who received him, to those who believed in his name, he gave the right to become children of God' (John 1:11,12). These verses show that there were some who received Him and some who did not. Have you ever received Jesus Christ as your personal Savior?"

The same illustration may be used to explain how the Christian lives in Christ (see Rom. 6:3-5; 8:1). The dollar bill represents the Christian and the Bible represents Christ. If I hand the Bible to you, and you accept it, you are also accepting the dollar that is in it. Likewise, if we are in Jesus Christ, and God accepts Christ, then we are also accepted by God.

The Kitten and the Puppies. Once upon a time there

was an orphaned kitten who was adopted and raised by a mother dog and her puppies. The kitten had a lot in common with her new family. The puppies had black and white spots and black noses; so did the kitten. The puppies had long tails and perky ears; the kitten did too. The puppies and the kitten all nursed on the mother's milk, slept in the same box and played with the same toys.

When the kitten and puppies were bigger, their mother taught them to bark. The puppies yipped and yapped, but the kitten could only meow. The mother taught them to fetch sticks, but the kitten could only paw at a butterfly. The mother taught them to wag their tails, but the kitten just curled into a ball and purred.

Was the kitten a dog? No! She grew up with dogs; she ate, slept and played with dogs all her life. In some ways she even looked and acted like a dog. But in order to *be* a dog, the kitten would have to be been born a dog.

In the same way, you may be a member of a church, and you may talk, look and act like a Christian. But looking and acting like a Christian doesn't make you a Christian. The only way to become a Christian is to be born a Christian (see John 3:1-8). It is impossible for a cat to be born again as a dog, but it *is* possible for sinners to be born again as Christians.

Baseball Facts and Feelings. Sometimes new Christians are confused by the conflict between the facts and feelings of their faith. We cannot always trust our feelings because they can change from one moment to the next. You can be the happiest fan in the baseball stadium when your team takes a one-run lead in the top of the ninth inning. But your feelings can take a dive when the opposing team scores two runs in the bottom of the ninth and wins the game. Feelings can change from inning to inning and from pitch to pitch. But the facts are recorded forever in the record book. The facts alone remain true.

In the same way we must put our faith in the *fact* that we have been made right with God through faith in Jesus Christ, even when we don't *feel* righteous.

The Ship and the Whip. Long ago a sailing ship was driven off course during a storm. Water and food supplies ran low as the captain fruitlessly searched for land. He announced to the passengers that anyone stealing water would be punished with 40 lashes.

A few days later the first officer reported to the captain that someone had been caught stealing water. The captain ordered the whipping, but the first officer protested. "The thief is your mother."

The captain loved his mother, but he knew that justice must be carried out. He called the passengers and crew together to explain that a theft had occurred and the punishment must be given. Then he stripped off his shirt and received the 40 lashes in his mother's place.

Because of our sin we deserve punishment. But Christ loved us while we were still sinners and He took the punishment in our place (see Rom. 5:8).

Answering Your Friend's Questions

Often when you are presenting the gospel to your friends, they may interrupt your presentation with questions. Sometimes their questions are relevant to the point, but often they only steer away from the main track of the presentation. The tips below will help you respond to questions so that your basic message may still be presented and heard.

Affirm and Defer

When your friend asks a good question, but which is off the main point, you may say: "Friend, that's a good question. It shows that you are thinking seriously about what I am saying. But may I defer answering it until after we have looked at a few more verses?"

It is important to affirm the value of the question while deferring your answer until your basic presentation is completed. But don't forget to deal with the question at the appropriate time.

Yes, But . . . When your friend's questions or comments show that he or she disagrees with your presentation or theology, you may say: "Yes, friend, I see your point. We can still look at these passages of Scriptures together and discover what the Scriptures have to say. And if you disagree with me or with what the Scriptures say, that's okay. But let's agree to disagree agreeably.

"Even Christians do not always agree on everything. But we do agree on what it means to believe in Jesus Christ. I would like to focus on that particular point by examining several more Bible passages with you."

I Don't Know, But . . . When your friend asks a question you cannot answer, you may say: "I don't know the answer to that question, but I'll be glad to do some homework on it and get back to you about it. But there is one thing I do know, and that is how one can know God personally by faith. I would like to talk to you about it for a moment."

Some of your friends may have sincere questions of a deep theological nature that you are unable to answer. Often it is best to refer your friend to books which deal thoroughly with the subject under question. Ask your pas-

tor or another mature Christian to suggest appropriate
resources that you may pass on to your friend.

Information and Questions. When your friend's questions or comments reveal that he or she doesn't believe
the Bible, you may say: "Friend, I respect your belief. My
desire is not to argue with you. Let me simply inform you
that one of the themes of the Bible is how a person can
know God personally. My question is, do you understand
what the Bible says about how a person can know God
personally?"

If your friend insists he or she does not believe a person can know God personally, you may say: "I am not asking what you *believe* about the Bible, but what you *understand* the Bible to say about how a person can know God
personally."

Often a person who does not believe the Bible misun-
derstands what the Bible says about knowing God personally. After your friend answers, ask if you may present
clearly what the Bible *does* say so he or she can make an
informed decision about accepting or rejecting the Bible's
message.

Affirm and Challenge. Some of your friends may identify themselves as atheists or agnostics. "Atheist" literally
means "no God," indicating that the individual *knows* that
God does *not* exist. "Agnostic" literally means "no knowledge," reflecting that the individual *does not know* whether
God exists or not.

Affirm and challenge your agnostic friends by saying:
"I respect your position and I don't want to argue with
you. But I have found something which has convinced me
that God exists and has helped me know God personally.
May I share with you what I know so you can make your

own decision about it?"

Affirm your atheist friends in a similar way. Then challenge them by saying: "A true atheist *knows* that God does not and cannot exist. Are you saying that you have acquired the totality of universal knowledge and know conclusively that God does not and cannot exist?" Only a fool would claim to know everything, so your friend must admit that his atheism extends only as far as his present knowledge.

Then ask: "Friend, is it possible that God might exist outside your limited knowledge?" If your friend is honest he or she will agree that God may exist but he or she doesn't know it. Your atheist is now an agnostic, so move to the agnostic approach above. (See Rom. 1:16-20 for some interesting insights on what everybody knows about God.)

Let's See What the Bible Says. It is always best to answer questions, comments or objections directly from the Bible. You may say: "Friend, that's a good question. Let's see what the Bible says about it." For example:

- "There are hypocrites in the church" (see Rom. 3:21-23; 7; 8).
- "What about the heathen who have never heard the gospel?" (see Rom. 2:11-16).
- "I've always been a Christian" (see Rom. 3:21-23; 5:8-11).
- "A God of love would never send anyone to hell" (see John 1:11,12; 3:16-21; Rom. 1:21-32; 10:12-21).
- "I don't believe Christ is the only way" (see John 14:6; Acts 4:12; 2 Cor. 5:17—6:2).
- "I believe that I must also do something in

order to go to heaven" (see Rom. 1:17;
3:19,20; Eph. 2:8,9).

A very helpful book for answering tough question is
Hard Questions, edited by Frank Colquhoun (InterVarsity
Press).

Examples of Commitment and Relationship

The President Example. If your friend is struggling
with the concept of knowing God personally, you may say:
"Let's compare knowing Christ to knowing the president
of the United States. We know what the president looks
like and we know the names of his family members. We
know something about his background and we know that
he lives in the White House. But have you ever met the
president of the United States personally? No? Neither
have I!

"There is a great difference between *knowing about*
Jesus Christ and *knowing Him personally*. Being a Christian means you know Christ personally. Do you know Him
personally? Would you like to open your life to Him and
begin a personal relationship with Him?"

The Marriage Example. When your friends reveal that
they don't understand what it means to make a commitment to Christ, you may say: "Making a Christian commitment is very much like getting married. A couple first
becomes acquainted and their relationship grows through
dating. Finally they realize that they need each other and
they decide to get married.

"During the wedding ceremony they make definite commitments to each other 'for better or worse, for richer or poorer.' Their close relationship is now confirmed through their formal statements of commitment 'till death do us part.'

"Becoming a Christian is a lot like the marriage relationship. A person first becomes acquainted with Jesus Christ, who He is and what He did. Finally that person realizes that he needs Jesus Christ as his personal Savior and Lord, and decides to commit his life to Christ. Your relationship to Christ only becomes definite when you personally commit your life to Christ. Have you established a personal relationship with Christ by committing your life to Him? Would you like to pray a prayer of commitment now?"

Sources and Resources

Pamphlets and Tracts. *The ABCs of Christianity*, The Vine Publishers, 5742 Hamilton Ave., Cincinnati, OH 45224. For youth and adults.

Ajuda (Portuguese), *Au Secours* (French), *Soccorro* (Spanish), The Vine Publishers, 5742 Hamilton Ave., Cincinnati, OH 45224.

The Bridge to Life, NavPress, P.O. Box 1659, Colorado Springs, CO 80901. For use with junior high and high school youth. Also can be used with the elderly and visually impaired because of its large print and pictures.

The Four Spiritual Laws, Campus Crusade for Christ International, San Bernardino, CA 92404. For high school, college age and adults.

The Good News Glove, Campus Crusade for Christ

International, San Bernardino, CA 92404. For use with
children from age four to eight.

Books. Frank Colquhoun. *Four Portraits of Jesus*. Downers Grove, IL: InterVarsity Press, 1985.
Harvie Conn. *Evangelism: Doing Justice & Preaching Grace*. Grand Rapids, MI: Zondervan Publishing House, 1982.
W. Phillip Keller. *A Layman Looks at the Lamb of God*. Minneapolis: Bethany House Publishers, 1982.
Robert Munger. *My Heart—Christ's Home*. Downer's Grove, IL: InterVarsity Press, 1986.
Joyce Neville. *How to Share Your Faith Without Being Offensive*. New York: Winston-Seabury Press, 1983.
R C. Sproul. *Basic Training: Plain Talk on the Key Truths of the Faith*. Grand Rapids, MI: Zondervan Publishing House, 1982.
C. Peter Wagner. *Your Spiritual Gifts Can Help Your Church Grow*. Ventura, CA: Regal Books, 1979).